The Splendid Spur

Arthur Thomas Quiller-Couch

THE SPLENDID SPUR

TO

EDWARD GWYNNE EARDLEY-WILMOT.

MY DEAR EDDIE,

Whatever view a story-teller may take of his business, 'tis happy when he can think, "This book of mine will please such and such a friend," and may set that friend's name after the title page. For even if to please (as some are beginning to hold) should be no part of his aim, at least 'twill always be a reward: and (in unworthier moods) next to a Writer I would choose to be a Lamplighter, as the only other that gets so cordial a "God bless him!" in the long winter evenings.

To win such a welcome at such a time from a new friend or two would be the happiest fortune for my tale. But to you I could wish it to speak particularly, seeing that under the coat of JACK MARVEL *beats the heart of your friend*

Q.

Torquay, August 22d, 1889.

INTRODUCTORY NOTE.

"Q."

A year or two ago it was observed that three writers were using the curiously popular signature "Q." This was hardly less confusing than that one writer should use three signatures (Grant Allen, Arbuthnot Wilson, and Anon), but as none of the three was willing to try another letter, they had to leave it to the public (whose decision in such matters is final) to say who is Q to it. The public said, Let him wear this proud letter who can win it, and for the present at least it is in the possession of the author of "The Splendid Spur" and "The Blue Pavilions." It would seem, too, as if it were his "to keep," for "Q" is like the competition cups that are only yours for a season, unless you manage to carry them three times in succession. Mr. Quiller-Couch has been champion Q since 1890.

The interesting question is not so much, What has he done to be the only prominent Q of these years, as Is he to be the Q of all time? If so, he will do better work than he has yet done, though several of his latest sketches—and one in particular—are of very uncommon merit. Mr. Quiller-Couch is so unlike Mr. Kipling that one immediately wants to compare them. They are both young, and they have both shown such promise that it will be almost sad if neither can write a book to live—as, of course, neither has done as yet. Mr. Kipling is the more audacious, which is probably a matter of training. He was brought up in India, where one's beard grows much quicker than at Oxford, and where you not only become a man (and a cynic) in a hurry, but see and hear strange things (and print them) such as the youth of Oxford miss, or, becoming acquainted with, would not dare insert in the local magazine of the moment. So Mr. Kipling's first work betokened a knowledge of the world that is by no means to be found in "Dead Man's Rock," the first book published by Mr. Quiller-Couch. On the other hand, it cannot truly be said that Mr. Kipling's latest work is stronger than his first, while the other writer's growth is the most remarkable thing about him. It is precisely the same Mr. Kipling who is now in the magazines that was writing some years ago in India (and a rare good Mr. Kipling too), but the Mr. Quiller-Couch of to-day is the Quiller-Couch of "Dead Man's Rock" grown out of recognition. To compare their styles is really to compare the men. Mr. Kipling's is the more startling, the stronger (as yet), and the more mannered. Mark Twain, it appears, said he reads Mr. Kipling for his style, which is really the same thing as saying you read him for his books, though the American seems only to have meant that he eats the beef because he likes the salt. It is a journalistic style, aiming too constantly at sharp effects, always succeeding in getting them. Sometimes this is contrived at the expense of grammar, as when (a common trick with the author) he ends a story with such a paragraph as "Which is manifestly unfair." Mr. Quiller-Couch has never sinned in this way, but his first style was somewhat turgid, even melodramatic, and, compared with Mr. Kipling's, lacked distinction. From the beginning Mr. Kipling had the genius for using the right word twice in three times (Mr. Stevenson only misses it about once in twelve), while Mr. Quiller-Couch not only used the wrong word, but weighted it with adjectives. The charge, however, cannot be brought against him to-day, for having begun by writing like a Mr. Haggard not quite sure of himself (if one can imagine such a Mr. Haggard), and changing to an obvious imitation of Mr. Stevenson, he seems now to have made a style for himself. It is clear and careful, but not as yet strong winged. Its distinctive feature is that it is curiously musical.

"Dead Man's Rock" is a capital sensational story to be read and at once forgotten. It was followed by "The Astonishing History of Troy Town," which was humorous, and proved that the author owed a debt to Dickens. But it was not sufficiently humorous to be remarkable for its humor, and it will go hand in hand with "Dead Man's Rock" to oblivion. Until "The Splendid Spur" appeared Mr. Quiller-Couch had done little to suggest that an artist had joined the ranks of the story-tellers. It is not in anyway a great work, but it was among the best dozen novels of its year, and as the production of a new writer it was one of the most notable. About the same time was published another historical romance of the second class (for to nothing short of Sir Walter shall we give a first-class in this department), "Micah Clarke," by Mr. Conan Doyle. It was as inevitable that the two books should be compared as that he who enjoyed the one should enjoy the other. In one respect "Micah Clarke" is the better story. It contains one character, a soldier of fortune, who is more memorable than any single figure in "The Splendid Spur." This, however, is effected at a cost, for this man is the book. It contains, indeed, two young fellows, one of them a John Ridd, but no Diana Vernon would blow a kiss to either. Both stories are weak in pathos, despite Joan, but there are a score of humorous situations in "The Splendid Spur" that one could not forget if he would—which he would not—as, for instance, where hero and heroine are hidden in barrels in a ship, and hero cries through his bunghole, "Wilt marry me, sweetheart?" to which heroine replies, "Must get out of this cask first." Better still is the scene in which Captain Billy expatiates, with a mop and a bucket, on the merits of his crew. But the passages are for reading, not for hearing about. Of the characters, this same Captain Billy is not the worst, but perhaps the best is Joan, Mr. Quiller-Couch's first successful picture of a girl. A capital eccentric figure is killed (some good things are squandered in this book) just when we are beginning to find him a genuine novelty. Anything that is ready to leap into danger seems to be thought good enough for the hero of a fighting romance, so that Jack Marvel will pass (though

Delia, as is right and proper, is worth two of him, despite her coming-on disposition). The villain is a failure, and the plot poor. Nevertheless there are some ingenious complications in it. Jack's escape by means of the hangman's rope, which was to send him out of the world in a few hours, is a fine rollicking bit of sensation. Where Mr. Quiller-Couch and Mr. Conan Doyle both fail as compared with the great master of romance is in the introduction of historical figures and episodes. Scott would have been a great man if he had written no novel but "The Abbott" (one of his second best), and no part of "The Abbott" but the scene in which Mary signs away her crown. Mr. Quiller-Couch almost entirely avoids such attempts, and even Mr. Conan Doyle only dips into them timidly. There is, one has been told, a theory that the romancist has no right to picture history in this way. But he makes his rights when he does it as Scott did it.

Since "The Splendid Spur," Mr. Quiller-Couch has published nothing in book form which can be considered an advance on his best novel, but there have appeared by him a number of short Cornish sketches, which are perhaps best considered as experiments. They are perilously slight, and where they are successful one remembers them as sweet dreams or like a bar of music. All aim at this effect, so that many should not be taken at a time, and some (as was to be expected with such delicate work) miss their mark. It might be said that in several of these melodies Mr. Quiller-Couch has been writing the same thing again and again, determined to succeed absolutely, if not this time then the next, and if not the next time then the time after. In one case he has succeeded absolutely. "The Small People," is a prose "Song of the Shirt." To my mind this is a rare piece of work, and the biggest thing for its size that has been done in English fiction for some years.

These sketches have been called experiments. They show (as his books scarcely show) that Mr. Quiller-Couch can feel. They suggest that he may be able to do for Cornwall what Mr. Hardy has done for Dorset—though the methods of the two writers are as unlike as their counties. But that can only be if in filling his notebook with these little comedies and tragedies Mr. Quiller-Couch is preparing for more sustained efforts.

"Our hope and heart is with thee
We will stand and mark."

J. M. BARRIE.

CONTENTS

CHAPTER

I. THE BOWLING-GREEN OF THE "CROWN." 17

II. THE YOUNG MAN IN THE CLOAK OF
AMBER SATIN 24

III. I FIND MYSELF IN A TAVERN BRAWL: AND
BARELY ESCAPE. 31

IV. I TAKE THE ROAD. 44

V. MY ADVENTURE AT THE "THREE CUPS." 56

VI. THE FLIGHT IN THE PINE WOOD. 68

VII. I FIND A COMRADE. 77

VIII. I LOSE THE KING'S LETTER; AND AM CARRIED
TO BRISTOL. 86

IX. I BREAK OUT OF PRISON. 98

X. CAPTAIN POTTERY AND CAPTAIN SETTLE. 118

XI. I RIDE DOWN INTO TEMPLE: AND AM WELL
TREATED THERE 129

XII. HOW JOAN SAVED THE ARMY OF THE WEST;
AND SAW THE FIGHT ON BRADDOCK DOWN 137

XIII. I BUY A LOOKING GLASS AT BODMIN FAIR:
AND MEET WITH MR. HANNIBAL TINGCOMB. 146

XIV. I DO NO GOOD IN THE HOUSE OF GLEYS. 154

XV. I LEAVE JOAN AND RIDE TO THE WARS. 162

XVI. THE BATTLE OF STAMFORD HEATH. 170

XVII. I MEET WITH A HAPPY ADVENTURE BY BURNING
OF A GREEN LIGHT. 180

XVIII.   JOAN DOES ME HER LAST SERVICE............................193
XIX.   THE ADVENTURE OF THE HEARSE..........................205
XX.   THE ADVENTURE OF THE LEDGE; AND HOW I
         SHOOK HANDS WITH MY COMRADE........................217

CHAPTER I.

THE BOWLING-GREEN OF
THE "CROWN."

He that has jilted the Muse, forsaking her gentle pipe to follow the drum and trumpet, shall fruitlessly besiege her again when the time comes to sit at home and write down his adventures. 'Tis her revenge, as I am extremely sensible: and methinks she is the harder to me, upon reflection how near I came to being her lifelong servant, as you are to hear.

'Twas on November 29th, Ao. 1642—a clear, frosty day—that the King, with the Prince of Wales (newly recovered of the measles), the Princes Rupert and Maurice, and a great company of lords and gentlemen, horse and foot, came marching back to us from Reading. I was a scholar of Trinity College in Oxford at that time, and may begin my history at three o'clock on the same afternoon, when going (as my custom was) to Mr. Rob. Drury for my fencing lesson, I found his lodgings empty.

They stood at the corner of Ship Street, as you turn into the Corn Market—a low wainscoted chamber, ill-lighted but commodious. "He is off to see the show," thought I as I looked about me; and finding an easy cushion in the window, sat down to await him. Where presently, being tired out (for I had been carrying a halberd all day with the scholars' troop in Magdalen College Grove), and in despite of the open lattice, I fell sound asleep.

It must have been an hour after that I awoke with a chill (as was natural), and was stretching out a hand to pull the window close, but suddenly sat down again and fell to watching instead.

The window look'd down, at the height of ten feet or so, upon a bowling-green at the back of the "Crown" Tavern (kept by John Davenant, in the Corn Market), and across it to a rambling wing of the same inn; the fourth side—that to my left—being but an old wall, with a broad sycamore growing against it. 'Twas already twilight; and in the dark'ning house, over the green, was now one casement brightly lit, the curtains undrawn, and within a company of noisy drinkers round a table. They were gaming, as was easily told by their clicking of the dice and frequent oaths: and anon the bellow of some tipsy chorus would come across. 'Twas one of these catches, I dare say, that woke me: only just now my eyes were bent, not toward the singers, but on the still lawn between us.

The sycamore, I have hinted, was a broad tree, and must, in summer, have borne a goodly load of leaves: but now, in November, these were strewn thick over the green, and nothing left but stiff, naked boughs. Beneath it lay a crack'd bowl or two on the rank turf, and against the trunk a garden bench rested, I suppose for the convenience of the players. On this a man was now seated.

He was reading in a little book; and this first jogged my curiosity: for 'twas unnatural a man should read print at this dim hour, or, if he had a mind to try, should choose a cold bowling-green for his purpose. Yet he seemed to study his volume very attentively, but with a sharp look, now and then, toward the lighted window, as if the revellers disturb'd him. His back was partly turn'd to me; and what with this and the growing dusk, I could but make a guess at his face: but a plenty of silver hair fell over his fur collar, and his shoulders were bent a great deal. I judged him between fifty and sixty. For the rest, he wore a dark, simple suit, very straitly cut, with an ample furr'd cloak, and a hat rather tall, after the fashion of the last reign.

Now, why the man's behavior so engaged me, I don't know: but at the end of half an hour I was still watching him. By this, 'twas near dark, bitter cold, and his pretence to read mere fondness: yet he persevered—though with longer glances at the casement above, where the din at times was fit to wake the dead.

And now one of the dicers upsets his chair with a curse, and gets on his feet. Looking up, I saw his features for a moment—a slight, pretty boy, scarce above eighteen, with fair curls and flush'd cheeks like a girl's. It made me admire to see him in this ring of purple, villainous faces. 'Twas evident he was a young gentleman of quality, as well by his bearing as his handsome cloak of amber satin barr'd with black. "I think the devil's in these dice!" I heard him crying, and a pretty hubbub all about him: but presently the drawer enters with more wine, and he sits down quietly to a fresh game.

As soon as 'twas started, one of the crew, that had been playing but was now dropp'd out, lounges up from his seat, and coming to the casement pushes it open for fresh air. He was one that till now had sat in full view—a tall bully, with a gross pimpled nose; and led the catches in a bull's voice. The rest of the players paid no heed to his rising; and very soon his shoulders hid them, as he lean'd out, drawing in the cold breath.

During the late racket I had forgot for a while my friend under the sycamore, but now, looking that way, to my astonishment I saw him risen from his bench and stealing across to the house opposite. I say "stealing," for he kept all the way to the darker shadow of the wall, and besides had a curious trailing motion with his left foot as though the ankle of it had been wrung or badly hurt.

As soon as he was come beneath the window he stopped and called softly—

"Hist!"

The bully gave a start and look'd down. I could tell by this motion he did not look to find anyone in the bowling-green at that hour. Indeed he had been watching the shaft of light thrown past him by the room behind, and now moved so as to let it fall on the man that addressed him.

The other stands close under the window, as if to avoid this, and calls again—

"Hist!" says he, and beckons with a finger.

The man at the window still held his tongue (I suppose because those in the room would hear him if he spoke), and so for a while the two men studied one another in silence, as if considering their next moves.

After a bit, however, the bully lifted a hand, and turning back into the lighted room, walks up to one of the players, speaks a word or two and disappears.

I sat up on the window seat, where till now I had been crouching for fear the shaft of light should betray me, and presently (as I was expecting) heard the latch of the back perch gently lifted, and spied the heavy form of the bully coming softly over the grass.

Now, I would not have my readers prejudiced, and so may tell them this was the first time in my life I had played the eavesdropper. That I did so now I can never be glad enough, but 'tis true, nevertheless, my conscience pricked me; and I was even making a motion to withdraw when that occurred which would have fixed any man's attention, whether he wish'd it or no.

The bully must have closed the door behind him but carelessly, for hardly could he take a dozen steps when it opened again with a scuffle, and the large house dog belonging to the "Crown" flew at his heels with a vicious snarl and snap of the teeth.

'Twas enough to scare the coolest. But the fellow turn'd as if shot, and before he could snap again, had gripped him fairly by the throat. The struggle that follow'd I could barely see, but I heard the horrible sounds of it—the hard, short breathing of the man, the hoarse rage working in the dog's throat—and it turned me sick. The dog—a mastiff—was fighting now to pull loose, and the pair swayed this way and that in the dusk, panting and murderous.

I was almost shouting aloud—feeling as though 'twere my own throat thus gripp'd—when the end came. The man had his legs planted well apart.

I saw his shoulders heave up and bend as he tightened the pressure of his fingers; then came a moment's dead silence, then a hideous gurgle, and the mastiff dropped back, his hind legs trailing limp.

The bully held him so for a full minute, peering close to make sure he was dead, and then without loosening his hold, dragged him across the grass under my window. By the sycamore he halted, but only to shift his hands a little; and so, swaying on his hips, sent the carcase with a heave over the wall. I heard it drop with a thud on the far side.

During this fierce wrestle—which must have lasted about two minutes—the clatter and shouting of the company above had gone on without a break; and all this while the man with the white hair had rested quietly on one side, watching. But now he steps up to where the bully stood mopping his face (for all the coolness of the evening), and, with a finger between the leaves of his book, bows very politely.

"You handled that dog, sir, choicely well," says he, in a thin voice that seemed to have a chuckle hidden in it somewhere.

The other ceased mopping to get a good look at him.

"But sure," he went on, "'twas hard on the poor cur, that had never heard of Captain Lucius Higgs—"

I thought the bully would have had him by the windpipe and pitched him after the mastiff, so fiercely he turn'd at the sound of this name. But the old gentleman skipped back quite nimbly and held up a finger.

"I'm a man of peace. If another title suits you better—"

"Where the devil got you that name?" growled the bully, and had half a mind to come on again, but the other put in briskly—

"I'm on a plain errand of business. No need, as you hint, to mention names; and therefore let me present myself as Mr. Z. The residue of the alphabet is at your service to pick and choose from."

"My name is Luke Settle," said the big man hoarsely (but whether this was his natural voice or no I could not tell).

"Let us say 'Mr. X.' I prefer it."

The old gentleman, as he said this, popped his head on one side, laid the forefinger of his right hand across the book, and seem'd to be considering.

"Why did you throttle that dog a minute ago?" he asked sharply.

"Why, to save my skin," answers the fellow, a bit puzzled.

"Would you have done it for fifty pounds?"

"Aye, or half that."

"And how if it had been a *puppy*, Mr. X?"

Now all this from my hiding I had heard very clearly, for they stood right under me in the dusk. But as the old gentleman paused to let his question sink in, and the bully to catch the drift of it before answering, one of the dicers above struck up to sing a catch—

> "With a hey, trolly-lolly! a leg to the Devil,
> And answer him civil, and off with your cap:
> Sing—Hey, trolly-lolly! Good-morrow, Sir Evil,
>   We've finished the tap,
> And, saving your worship, we care not a rap!"

While this din continued, the stranger held up one forefinger again, as if beseeching silence, the other remaining still between the pages of his book.

"Pretty boys!" he said, as the noise died away; "pretty boys! 'Tis easily seen they have a bird to pluck."

"He's none of my plucking."

"And if he were, why not? Sure you've picked a feather or two before now in the Low Countries—hey?"

"I'll tell you what," interrupts the big man, "next time you crack one of your death's-head jokes, over the wall you go after the dog. What's to prevent it?"

"Why, this," answers the old fellow, cheerfully. "There's money to be made by doing no such thing. And I don't carry it all about with me. So, as 'tis late, we'd best talk business at once."

They moved away toward the seat under the sycamore, and now their words reached me no longer—only the low murmur of their voices or (to be correct) of the elder man's: for the other only spoke now and then, to put a question, as it seemed. Presently I heard an oath rapped out and saw the bully start up. "Hush, man!" cried the other, and "hark-ye now—"; so he sat down again. Their very forms were lost within the shadow. I, myself, was cold enough by this time and had a cramp in one leg—but lay still, nevertheless. And after awhile they stood up together, and came pacing across the bowling-green, side by side, the older man trailing his foot painfully to keep step. You may be sure I strain'd my ears.

"—besides the pay," the stranger was saying, "there's all you can win of this young fool, Anthony, and all you find on the pair, which I'll wager—"

They passed out of hearing, but turned soon, and came back again. The big man was speaking this time.

"I'll be shot if I know what game *you're* playing in this."

The elder chuckled softly. "I'll be shot if I mean you to," said he.

And this was the last I heard. For now there came a clattering at the door behind me, and Mr. Robert Drury reeled in, hiccuping a maudlin ballad about *Tib and young Colin, one fine day, beneath the haycock shade-a,* &c., &c., and cursing to find his fire gone out, and all in darkness. Liquor was ever his master, and to-day the King's health had been a fair excuse. He did not spy me, but the roar of his ballad had startled the two men outside, and so, while he was stumbling over chairs, and groping for a tinder-box, I slipp'd out in the darkness, and downstairs into the street.

CHAPTER II.

THE YOUNG MAN IN THE CLOAK OF AMBER SATIN,

Guess, any of you, if these events disturbed my rest that night. 'Twas four o'clock before I dropp'd asleep in my bed in Trinity, and my last thoughts were still busy with the words I had heard. Nor, on the morrow, did it fair any better with me: so that, at rhetoric lecture, our president—Dr. Ralph Kettle—took me by the ears before the whole class. He was the fiercer upon me as being older than the gross of my fellow-scholars, and (as he thought) the more restless under discipline. "A tutor'd adolescence," he would say, "is a fair grace before meat," and had his hourglass enlarged to point the moral for us. But even a rhetoric lecture must have an end, and so, tossing my gown to the porter, I set off at last for Magdalen Bridge, where the new barricado was building, along the Physic Garden, in front of East Gate.

The day was dull and low'ring, though my wits were too busy to heed the sky; but scarcely was I past the small gate in the city wall when a brisk shower of hail and sleet drove me to shelter in the Pig Market (or *Proscholium*) before the Divinity School. 'Tis an ample vaulted passage, as I dare say you know; and here I found a great company of people already driven by the same cause.

To describe them fully 'twould be necessary to paint the whole state of our city in those distracted times, which I have neither wit nor time for. But here, to-day, along with many doctors and scholars, were walking courtiers, troopers, mountebanks, cut-purses, astrologers, rogues and gamesters; together with many of the first ladies and gentlemen of England, as the Prince Maurice, the lords Andover, Digby and Colepepper, my lady Thynne, Mistress Fanshawe, Mr. Secretary Nicholas, the famous Dr. Harvey, arm-in-arm with my lord Falkland (whose boots were splash'd with mud, he having ridden over from his house at Great Tew), and many such, all mix'd in this incredible tag-rag. Mistress Fanshawe, as I remember, was playing on a lute, which she carried always slung about her shoulders: and close beside her, a fellow impudently puffing his specific against the *morbus campestris*, which already had begun to invade us.

"*Who'll buy?*" he was bawling. "'*Tis from the receipt of a famous Italian, and never yet failed man, woman, nor child, unless the heart were clean drown'd in the disease: the lest part of it good muscadine, and has virtue against the plague, smallpox, or surfeits!*"

I was standing before this jackanapes, when I heard a stir in the crowd behind me, and another calling, "*Who'll buy? Who'll buy?*"

Turning, I saw a young man, very gaily dressed, moving quickly about at the far end of the Pig Market, and behind him an old lackey, bent double with the weight of two great baskets that he carried. The baskets were piled with books, clothes, and gewgaws of all kinds; and 'twas the young gentleman that hawked his wares himself. "*What d'ye lack?*" he kept shouting, and would stop to unfold his merchandise, holding up now a book, and now a silk doublet, and running over their merits like any huckster—but with the merriest conceit in the world.

And yet 'twas not this that sent my heart flying into my mouth at the sight of him. For by his curls and womanish face, no less than the amber cloak with the black bars, I knew him at once for the same I had seen yesterday among the dicers.

As I stood there, drawn this way and that by many reflections, he worked his way through the press, selling here and there a trifle from his baskets, and at length came to a halt in front of me.

"Ha!" he cried, pulling off his plumed hat, and bowing low, "a scholar, I perceive. Let me serve you, sir. Here is the 'History of Saint George,'" and he picked out a thin brown quarto and held it up; "written by Master Peter Heylin; a ripe book they tell me (though, to be sure, I never read beyond the title), and the price a poor two shillings."

Now, all this while I was considering what to do. So, as I put my hand in my pocket, and drew out the shillings, I said very slowly, looking him in the eyes (but softly, so that the lackey might not hear)—

"So thus you feed your expenses at the dice: and my shilling, no doubt, is for Luke Settle, as well as the rest."

For the moment, under my look, he went white to the lips; then clapped his hand to his sword, withdrew it, and answered me, red as a turkey-cock—

"Shalt be a parson, yet, Master Scholar: but art in a damn'd hurry, it seems."

Now, I had ever a quick temper, and as he turned on his heel, was like to have replied and raised a brawl. My own meddling tongue had brought the rebuff upon me: but yet my heart was hot as he walked away.

I was standing there and looking after him, turning over in my hand the "Life of Saint George," when my fingers were aware of a slip of paper between the pages. Pulling it out, I saw 'twas scribbled over with writing and figures, as follows:—

"Mr. Anthony Killigrew, his acct for Oct. 25th, MDCXLII.—*For herrings, 2d.; for coffie, 4d.; for scowring my coat, 6d.; at bowls, 5s. 10d.; for bleading me, 1s. 0d.; for ye King's speech, 3d.; for spic'd wine (with Marjory), 2s. 4d.; for seeing ye Rhinoceros, 4d.; at ye Ranter-go-round, 6 3/4d.; for a pair of silver buttons, 2s. 6d.; for apples, 2 1/2d.; for ale, 6d.; at ye dice, L17 5s.; for spic'd wine (again), 4s. 6d.*"

And so on.

As I glanced my eye down this paper, my anger oozed away, and a great feeling of pity came over me, not only at the name of Anthony—the name I had heard spoken in the bowling-green last night—but also to see that monstrous item of L17 odd spent on the dice. 'Twas such a boy, too, after all, that I was angry with, that had spent fourpence to see the rhinoceros at a fair, and rode on the ranter-go-round (with "Marjory," no doubt, as 'twas for her, no doubt, the silver buttons were bought). So that, with quick forgiveness, I hurried after him, and laid a hand on his shoulder.

He stood by the entrance, counting up his money, and drew himself up very stiff.

"I think, sir," said I, "this paper is yours."

"I thank you," he answered, taking it, and eyeing me. "Is there anything, besides, you wished to say?"

"A great deal, maybe, if your name be Anthony."

"Master Anthony Killigrew is my name, sir; now serving under Lord Bernard Stewart in His Majesty's troop of guards."

"And mine is Jack Marvel," said I.

"Of the Yorkshire Marvels?"

"Why, yes; though but a shoot of that good stock, transplanted to Cumberland, and there sadly withered."

"'Tis no matter, sir," said he politely; "I shall be proud to cross swords with you."

"Why, bless your heart!" I cried out, full of laughter at this childish punctilio; "d'ye think I came to fight you?"

"If not, sir"—and he grew colder than ever—"you are going a cursed roundabout way to avoid it."

Upon this, finding no other way out of it, I began my tale at once: but hardly had come to the meeting of the two men on the bowling-green, when he interrupts me politely—

"I think, Master Marvel, as yours is like to be a story of some moment, I will send this fellow back to my lodgings. He's a long-ear'd dog that I am saving from the gallows for so long as my conscience allows me. The shower is done, I see; so if you know of a retir'd spot, we will talk there more at our leisure."

He dismiss'd his lackey, and stroll'd off with me to the Trinity Grove, where, walking up and down, I told him all I had heard and seen the night before.

"And now," said I, "can you tell me if you have any such enemy as this white-hair'd man, with the limping gait?"

He had come to a halt, sucking in his lips and seeming to reflect—

"I know one man," he began: "but no—'tis impossible."

As I stood, waiting to hear more, he clapp'd his hand in mine, very quick and friendly: "Jack," he cried;—"I'll call thee Jack—'twas an honest good turn thou hadst in thy heart to do me, and I a surly rogue to think of fighting—I that could make mincemeat of thee."

"I can fence a bit," answer'd I.

"Now, say no more, Jack: I love thee."

He look'd in my face, still holding my hand and smiling. Indeed, there was something of the foreigner in his brisk graceful ways—yet not unpleasing. I was going to say I had never seen the like—ah, me! that both have seen and know the twin image so well.

"I think," said I, "you had better be considering what to do."

He laugh'd outright this time; and resting with his legs cross'd, against the trunk of an elm, twirl'd an end of his long lovelocks, and looked at me comically. Said he: "Tell me, Jack, is there aught in me that offends thee?"

"Why, no," I answered. "I think you're a very proper young man—such as I should loathe to see spoil'd by Master Settle's knife."

"Art not quick at friendship, Jack, but better at advising; only in this case fortune has prevented thy good offices. Hark ye," he lean'd forward and glanc'd to right and left, "if these twain intend my hurt—as indeed 'twould seem—they lose their labor: for this very night I ride from Oxford."

"And why is that?"

"I'll tell thee, Jack, tho' I deserve to be shot. I am bound with a letter from His Majesty to the Army of the West, where I have friends, for my father's sake—Sir Deakin Killigrew of Gleys, in Cornwall. 'Tis a sweet country, they say, tho' I have never seen it."

"Not seen thy father's country?"

"Why no—for he married a Frenchwoman, Jack, God rest her dear soul!"—he lifted his hat—"and settled in that country, near Morlaix, in Brittany, among my mother's kin; my grandfather refusing to see or speak with him, for wedding a poor woman without his consent. And in France was I born and bred, and came to England two years agone; and this last July the old curmudgeon died. So that my father, who was an only son, is even now in England returning to his estates: and with him my only sister Delia. I shall meet them on the way. To think of it!" (and I declare the tears sprang to his eyes): "Delia will be a woman grown, and ah! to see dear Cornwall together!"

Now I myself was only a child, and had been made an orphan when but nine years old, by the smallpox that visited our home in Wastdale Village, and carried off my father, the Vicar, and my dear mother. Yet his simple words spoke to my heart and woke so tender a yearning for the small stone cottage, and the bridge, and the grey fells of Yewbarrow above it, that a mist rose in my eyes too, and I turn'd away to hide it.

"'Tis a ticklish business," said I after a minute, "to carry the King's letter. Not one in four of his messengers comes through, they say. But since it keeps you from the dice—"

"That's true. To-night I make an end."

"To-night!"

"Why, yes. To-night I go for my revenge, and ride straight from the inn door."

"Then I go with you to the 'Crown,'" I cried, very positive.

He dropp'd playing with his curl, and look'd me in the face, his mouth twitching with a queer smile.

"And so thou shalt Jack: but why?"

"I'll give no reason," said I, and knew I was blushing.

"Then be at the corner of All Hallows' Church in Turl Street at seven to-night. I lodge over Master Simon's, the glover, and must be about my affairs. Jack,"—he came near and took my hand—"am sure thou lovest me."

He nodded, with another cordial smile, and went his way up the grove, his amber cloak flaunting like a belated butterfly under the leaf less trees; and so pass'd out of my sight.

CHAPTER III.

I FIND MYSELF IN A TAVERN BRAWL: AND BARELY ESCAPE.

It wanted, maybe, a quarter to seven, that evening, when, passing out at the College Gate on my way to All Hallows' Church, I saw under the lantern there a man loitering and talking with the porter. 'Twas Master Anthony's lackey; and as I came up, he held out a note for me.

Deare Jack

    Wee goe to the "Crowne" at VI. o'clock, I having mett with Captain Settle, who is on dewty with the horse tonite, and must to Abendonn by IX. I looke for you—

Your unfayned loving
A. K.

The bearer has left my servise, and his helth conserus me nott. Soe kik him if he tarrie.

This last advice I had no time to carry out with any thoroughness: but being put in a great dread by this change of hour, pelted off toward the Corn Market as fast as legs could take me, which was the undoing of a little round citizen into whom I ran full tilt at the corner of Balliol College: who, before I could see his face in the darkness, was tipp'd on his back in the gutter and using the most dismal expressions. So I left him, considering that my excuses would be unsatisfying to his present demands, and to his cooler judgment a superfluity.

The windows of the "Crown" were cheerfully lit behind their red blinds. A few straddling grooms and troopers talked and spat in the brightness of the entrance, and outside in the street was a servant leading up and down a beautiful sorrel mare, ready saddled, that was mark'd on the near hind leg with a high white stocking. In the passage, I met the host of the "Crown," Master John Davenant, and sure (I thought) in what odd corners will the Muse pick up her favorites! For this slow, loose-cheek'd vintner was no less than father to Will Davenant, our Laureate, and had belike read no other verse in his life but those at the bottom of his own pint-pots.

"Top of the stairs," says he, indicating my way, "and open the door ahead of you, if y'are the young gentleman Master Killigrew spoke of."

I had my foot on the bottom step, when from the room above comes the crash of a table upsetting, with a noise of broken glass, chairs thrust back, and a racket of outcries. Next moment, the door was burst open, letting out a flood of light and curses; and down flies a drawer, three steps at a time, with a red stain of wine trickling down his white face.

"Murder!" he gasped out; and sitting down on a stair, fell to mopping his face, all sick and trembling.

I was dashing past him, with the landlord at my heels, when three men came tumbling out at the door, and downstairs. I squeezed myself against the wall to let them pass: but Master Davenant was pitch'd to the very foot of the stairs. And then he picked himself up and ran out into the Corn Market, the drawer after him, and both shouting "Watch! Watch!" at the top of their lungs; and so left the three fellows to push by the women already gathered in the passage, and gain the street at their ease. All this happen'd while a man could count twenty; and in half a minute I heard the ring of steel and was standing in the doorway.

There was now no light within but what was shed by the fire and two tallow candles that gutter'd on the mantelshelf. The remaining candlesticks lay in a pool of wine on the floor, amid broken glasses, bottles, scattered coins, dice boxes and pewter pots. In the corner to my right cower'd a potboy, with tankard dangling in his hand, and the contents spilling into his shoes. His wide terrified eyes were fix'd on the far end of the room, where Anthony and the brute Settle stood, with a shatter'd chair between them. Their swords were cross'd in tierce, and grating together as each sought occasion for a lunge: which might have been fair enough but for a dog-fac'd trooper in a frowsy black periwig, who, as I enter'd, was gathering a handful of coins from under the fallen table, and now ran across, sword in hand, to the Captain's aid.

'Twas Anthony that fac'd me, with his heel against the wainscoting, and, catching my cry of alarm, he call'd out cheerfully over the Captain's shoulder, but without lifting his eyes—

"Just in time, Jack! Take off the second cur, that's a sweet boy!"

Now I carried no sword; but seizing the tankard from the potboy's hand, I hurl'd it at the dog-fac'd trooper. It struck him fair between the shoulder blades; and with a yell of pain he spun round and came toward me, his point glittering in a way that turn'd me cold. I gave back a pace, snatch'd up a chair (that luckily had a wooden seat) and with my back against the door, waited his charge.

'Twas in this posture that, flinging a glance across the room, I saw the Captain's sword describe a small circle of light, and next moment, with a sharp cry, Anthony caught at the blade, and stagger'd against the wall, pinn'd through the chest to the wainscoting.

"Out with the lights, Dick!" bawl'd Settle, tugging out his point. "Quick, fool—the window!"

Dick, with a back sweep of his hand, sent the candles flying off the shelf; and, save for the flicker of the hearth, we were in darkness. I felt, rather than saw, his rush toward me; leap'd aside; and brought down my chair with a crash on his skull. He went down like a ninepin, but scrambled up in a trice, and was running for the window.

There was a shout below as the Captain thrust the lattice open: another, and the two dark forms had clambered through the purple square of the casement, and dropped into the bowling-green below.

By this, I had made my way across the room, and found Anthony sunk against the wall, with his feet outstretched. There was something he held out toward me, groping for my hand and at the same time whispering in a thick, choking voice—

"Here, Jack, here: pocket it quick!"

'Twas a letter, and as my fingers closed on it they met a damp smear, the meaning of which was but too plain.

"Button it—sharp—in thy breast: now feel for my sword."

"First let me tend thy hurt, dear lad."

"Nay—quickly, my sword! 'Tis pretty, Jack, to hear thee say 'dear lad.' A cheat to die like this—could have laugh'd for years yet. The dice were cogg'd—hast found it?"

I groped beside him, found the hilt, and held it up.

"So—'tis thine, Jack: and my mare, Molly, and the letter to take. Say to Delia—Hark! they are on the stairs. Say to—"

With a shout the door was flung wide, and on the threshold stood the Watch, their lanterns held high and shining in Anthony's white face, and on the black stain where his doublet was thrown open.

In numbers they were six or eight, led by a small, wrynecked man that held a long staff, and wore a gilt chain over his furr'd collar. Behind, in the doorway, were huddled half a dozen women, peering: and Master Davenant at the back of all, his great face looming over their shoulders like a moon.

"Now, speak up, Master Short!"

"Aye, that I will—that I will: but my head is considering of affairs," answered Master Short—he of the wryneck. "One, two, three—" He look'd round the room, and finding but one capable of resisting (for the potboy was by this time in a fit), clear'd his throat, and spoke up—

"In the king's name, I arrest you all—so help me God! Now what's the matter?"

"Murder," said I, looking up from my work of staunching Anthony's wound.

"Then forbear, and don't do it."

"Why, Master Short, they've been forbearin' these ten minutes," a woman's voice put in.

"Hush, and hear Master Short: he knows the law, an' all the dubious maxims of the same."

"Aye, aye: he says forbear i' the King's name, which is to say, that other forbearing is neither law nor grace. Now then, Master Short!"

Thus exhorted, the man of law continued—

"I charge ye as honest men to disperse!"

"Odds truth, Master Short, why you've just laid 'em under arrest!"

"H'm, true: then let 'em stay so—in the king's name—and have done with it."

Master Short, in fact, was growing testy: but now the women push'd by him, and, by screaming at the sight of blood, put him out of all patience. Dragging them back by the skirts, he told me he must take the depositions, and pull'd out pen and ink horn.

"Sirs," said I, laying poor Anthony's head softly back, "you are too late: whilst ye were cackling my friend is dead."

"Then, young man, thou must come along."

"Come along?"

"The charge is *homocidium*, or manslaying, with or without malice prepense—"

"But—" I look'd round. The potboy was insensible, and my eyes fell on Master Davenant, who slowly shook his head.

"I'll say not a word," said he, stolidly: "lost twenty pound, one time, by a lawsuit."

"Pack of fools!" I cried, driven beyond endurance. "The guilty ones have escap'd these ten minutes. Now stop me who dares!"

And dashing my left fist on the nose of a watchman who would have seized me, I clear'd a space with Anthony's sword, made a run for the casement, and dropp'd out upon the bowling-green.

A pretty shout went up as I pick'd myself off the turf and rush'd for the back door. 'Twas unbarr'd, and in a moment I found myself tearing down the passage and out into the Corn Market, with a score or so tumbling downstairs at my heels, and yelling to stop me. Turning sharp to my right, I flew up Ship Street, and through the Turl, and doubled back up the High Street, sword in hand. The people I pass'd were too far taken aback, as I suppose, to interfere. But a many must have join'd in the chase: for presently the street behind me was thick with the clatter of footsteps and cries of "A thief—a thief! Stop him!"

At Quater Voies I turn'd again, and sped down toward St. Aldate's, thence to the left by Wild Boar Street, and into St. Mary's Lane. By this, the shouts had grown fainter, but were still following. Now I knew there was no possibility to get past the city gates, which were well guarded at night. My hope reach'd no further than the chance of outwitting the pursuit for a while longer. In the end I was sure the potboy's evidence would clear me, and therefore began to enjoy the fun. Even my certain expulsion from College on the morrow seem'd of a piece with the rest of events and (prospectively) a matter for laughter. For the struggle at the "Crown" had unhinged my wits, as I must suppose and you must believe, if you would understand my behavior in the next half hour.

A bright thought had struck me: and taking a fresh wind, I set off again round the corner of Oriel College, and down Merton Street toward Master Timothy Carter's house, my mother's cousin. This gentleman— who was town clerk to the Mayor and Corporation of Oxford—was also in a sense my guardian, holding it trust about L200 (which was all my inheritance), and spending the same jealously on my education. He was a very small, precise lawyer, about sixty years old, shaped like a pear, with a prodigious self-important manner that came of associating with great men: and all the knowledge I had of him was pick'd up on the rare occasions (about twice a year) that I din'd at his table. He had early married and lost an aged shrew, whose money had been the making of him: and had more respect for law and authority than any three men in Oxford. So that I reflected, with a kind of desperate hilarity, on the greeting he was like to give me.

This kinsman of mine had a fine house at the east end of Merton Street as you turn into Logic Lane: and I was ten yards from the front door, and running my fastest, when suddenly I tripp'd and fell headlong.

Before I could rise, a hand was on my shoulder, and a voice speaking in my ear—

"Pardon, comrade. We are two of a trade, I see."

'Twas a fellow that had been lurking at the corner of the lane, and had thrust out a leg as I pass'd. He was pricking up his ears now to the cries of "Thief—thief!" that had already reach'd the head of the street, and were drawing near.

"I am no thief," said I.

"Quick!" He dragged me into the shadow of the lane. "Hast a crown in thy pocket?"

"Why?"

"Why, for a good turn. I'll fog these gentry for thee. Many thanks, comrade," as I pull'd out the last few shillings of my pocket money. "Now pitch thy sword over the wall here, and set thy foot on my hand. 'Tis a rich man's garden, t'other side, that I was meaning to explore myself; but another night will serve."

"'Tis Master Carter's," said I; "and he's my kinsman."

"The devil!—but never mind, up with thee! Now mark a pretty piece of play. 'Tis pity thou shouldst be across the wall and unable to see."

He gave a great hoist: catching at the coping of the wall, I pull'd myself up and sat astride of it.

"Good turf below—ta-ta, comrade!"

By now, the crowd was almost at the corner. Dropping about eight feet on to good turf, as the fellow had said, I pick'd myself up and listen'd.

"Which way went he?" call'd one, as they came near.

"Down the street!" "No: up the lane!'" "Hush!" "Up the lane, I'll be sworn." "Here, hand the lantern!" &c., &c.

While they debated, my friend stood close on the other side of the wall: but now I heard him dash suddenly out, and up the lane for his life. "There he goes!" "Stop him!" the cries broke out afresh. "Stop him, i' the king's name!" The whole pack went pelting by, shouting, stumbling, swearing.

For two minutes or more the stragglers continued to hurry past by ones and twos. As soon as their shouts died away, I drew freer breath and look'd around.

I was in a small, turfed garden, well stock'd with evergreen shrubs, at the back of a tall house that I knew for Master Carter's. But what puzzled me was a window in the first floor, very brightly lit, and certain sounds issuing therefrom that had no correspondence with my kinsman's reputation.

> "It was a frog leap'd into a pool—
> Fol—de—riddle, went souse in the middle!
> Says he, This is better than moping in school.
> With a—"

"—Your Royal Highness, have some pity! What hideous folly! Oh, dear, dear—"

> "With a fa-la-tweedle-tweedle,
> Tiddifol-iddifol-ido!"

"—Your Royal Highness, I *cannot* sing the dreadful stuff! Think of my grey hairs!"

"Tush! Master Carter—nonsense; 'tis choicely well sung. Come, brother, the chorus!"

"With a fa-la—"

And the chorus was roar'd forth, with shouts of laughter and clinking of glasses. Then came an interval of mournful appeal, and my kinsman's voice was again lifted—

>"He scattered the tadpoles, and set 'em agog,
>Hey! nod-noddy-all head and no body!
>Oh, mammy! Oh, minky!—"

"—O, mercy, mercy! it makes me sweat for shame."

Now meantime I had been searching about the garden, and was lucky enough to find a tool shed, and inside of this a ladder hanging, which now I carried across and planted beneath the window. I had a shrewd notion of what I should find at the top, remembering now to have heard that the Princes Rupert and Maurice were lodging with Master Carter: but the truth beat all my fancies.

For climbing softly up and looking in, I beheld my poor kinsman perch'd on his chair a-top of the table, in the midst of glasses, decanters, and desserts: his wig askew, his face white, save where, between the eyes, a medlar had hit and broken, and his glance shifting wildly between the two princes, who in easy postures, loose and tipsy, lounged on either side of him, and beat with their glasses on the board.

"Bravissimo! More, Master Carter—more!"

>"O mammy, O nunky, here's cousin Jack Frog—
>With a fa-la—"

I lifted my knuckles and tapp'd on the pane; whereon Prince Maurice starts up with an oath, and coming to the window, flings it open.

"Pardon, your Highness," said I, and pull'd myself past him into the room, as cool as you please.

'Twas worth while to see their surprise. Prince Maurice ran back to the table for his sword: his brother (being more thoroughly drunk) dropped a decanter on the floor, and lay back staring in his chair. While as for my kinsman, he sat with mouth wide and eyes starting, as tho' I were a very ghost. In the which embarrassment I took occasion to say, very politely—

"Good evening, nunky!"

"Who the devil is this?" gasps Prince Rupert.

"Why the fact is, your Highnesses," answered I, stepping up and laying my sword on the table, while I pour'd out a glass, "Master Timothy Carter here is my guardian, and has the small sum of L200 in his possession for my use, of which I happen to-night to stand in immediate need. So you see—" I finished the sentence by tossing off a glass. "This is rare stuff!" I said.

"Blood and fury!" burst out Prince Rupert, fumbling for his sword, and then gazing, drunk and helpless.

"Two hundred pound! Thou jackanapes—" began Master Carter.

"I'll let you off with fifty to-night," said I.

"Ten thousand—!"

"No, fifty. Indeed, nunky," I went on, "'tis very simple. I was at the 'Crown' tavern—"

"At a tavern!"

"Aye, at a game of dice—"

"Dice!"

"Aye, and a young man was killed—"

"Thou shameless puppy! A man murder'd!"

"Aye, nunky; and the worst is they say 'twas I that kill'd him."

"He's mad. The boy's stark raving mad!" exclaim'd my kinsman. "To come here in this trim!"

"Why, truly, nunky, thou art a strange one to talk of appearances. Oh, dear!" and I burst into a wild fit of laughing, for the wine had warm'd me up to play the comedy out. "To hear thee sing

"'With a fa—la—tweedle—tweedle!'

and—Oh, nunky, that medlar on thy face is so funny!"

"In Heaven's name, stop!" broke in the Prince Maurice. "Am I mad, or only drunk? Rupert, if you love me, say I am no worse than drunk."

"Lord knows," answer'd his brother. "I for one was never this way before."

"Indeed, your Highnesses be only drunk," said I, "and able at that to sign the order that I shall ask you for."

"An order!"

"To pass the city gates to-night."

"Oh, stop him somebody," groan'd Prince Rupert: "my head is whirling."

"With your leave," I explain'd, pouring out another glassful: "tis the simplest matter, and one that a child could understand. You see, this young man was kill'd, and they charg'd me with it; so away I ran, and the Watch after me; and therefore I wish to pass the city gates. And as I may have far to travel, and gave my last groat to a thief for hoisting me over Master Carter's wall—"

"A thief—my wall!" repeated Master Carter. "Oh well is thy poor mother in her grave!"

"—Why, therefore I came for money," I wound up, sipping the wine, and nodding to all present.

'Twas at this moment that, catching my eye, the Prince Maurice slapp'd his leg, and leaning back, broke into peal after peal of laughter. And in a moment his brother took the jest also; and there we three sat and shook, and roar'd unquenchably round Master Carter, who, staring blankly from one to another, sat gaping, as though the last alarm were sounding in his ears.

"Oh! oh! oh! Hit me on the back, Maurice!"

"Oh! oh! I cannot—'tis killing me—Master Carter, for pity's sake, look not so; but pay the lad his money."

"Your Highness—"

"Pay it I say; pay it: 'tis fairly won."

"Fifty pounds!"

"Every doit," said I: "I'm sick of schooling."

"Be hang'd if I do!" snapp'd Master Carter.

"Then be hang'd, sir, but all the town shall hear to-morrow of the frog and the pool! No, sir: I am off to see the world—

"'Says he: "This is better than moping in school!"'"

"Your Highnesses," pleaded the unhappy man, "if, to please you, I sang that idiocy, which, for fifty years now, I had forgotten—"

"Exc'll'nt shong," says Prince Rupert, waking up; "less have't again!"

*   *   *   *

To be short, ten o'clock was striking from St. Mary's spire when, with a prince on either side of me, and thirty guineas in my pocket (which was all the loose gold he had), I walked forth from Master Carter's door. To make up the deficiency, their highnesses had insisted on furnishing me with a suit made up from the simplest in their joint wardrobes—riding-boots, breeches, buff-coat, sash, pistols, cloak, and feather'd hat, all of which fitted me excellently well. By the doors of Christ Church, before we came to the south gate, Prince Rupert, who had been staggering in his walk, suddenly pull'd up, and leaned against the wall.

"Why—odd's my life—we've forgot a horse for him!" he cried.

"Indeed, your Highness," I answered, "if my luck holds the same, I shall find one by the road." (How true this turned out you shall presently hear.)

There was no difficulty at the gate, where the sentry recogniz'd the two princes and open'd the wicket at once. Long after it had clos'd behind me, and I stood looking back at Oxford towers, all bath'd in the winter moonlight, I heard the two voices roaring away up the street:

"It was a frog leap'd into a pool—"

At length they died into silence; and, hugging the king's letter in my breast, I stepped briskly forward on my travels.

CHAPTER IV.

I TAKE THE ROAD.

So puffed up was I by the condescension of the two princes, and my head so busy with big thoughts, that not till I was over the bridges and climbing the high ground beyond South Hincksey, with a shrewd northeast wind at my back, could I spare time for a second backward look. By this, the city lay spread at my feet, very delicate and beautiful in a silver network, with a black clump or two to southward, where the line of Bagley trees ran below the hill. I pulled out the letter that Anthony had given me. In the moonlight the brown smear of his blood was plain to see, running across the superscription:

> *"To our trusty and well beloved Sir Ralph Hopton, at our Army in Cornwall—these."*

'Twas no more than I look'd for; yet the sight of it and the king's red seal, quicken'd my step as I set off again. And I cared not a straw for Dr. Kettle's wrath on the morrow.

Having no desire to fall in with any of the royal outposts that lay around Abingdon, I fetched well away to the west, meaning to shape my course for Faringdon, and so into the great Bath road. 'Tis not my purpose to describe at any length my itinerary, but rather to reserve my pen for those more moving events that overtook me later. Only in the uncertain light I must have taken a wrong turn to the left (I think near

Besselsleigh) that led me round to the south: for, coming about daybreak to a considerable town, I found it to be, not Faringdon, but Wantage. There was no help for it, so I set about enquiring for a bed. The town was full, and already astir with preparations for cattle-fair; and neither at the "Bear" nor the "Three Nuns" was there a bed to be had. But at length at the "Boot" tavern—a small house, I found one just vacated by a couple of drovers, and having cozen'd the chambermaid to allow me a clean pair of sheets, went upstairs very drowsily, and in five minutes was sleeping sound.

I awoke amid a clatter of voices, and beheld the room full of womankind.

"He's waking," said one.

"Tis a pity, too, to be afflicted thus—and he such a pretty young man!"

This came from the landlady, who stood close, her hand shaking my shoulder roughly.

"What's amiss?" I asked, rubbing my eyes.

"Why, 'tis three of the afternoon."

"Then I'll get up, as soon as you retire."

"Lud! we've been trying to wake thee this hour past; but 'twas sleep—sleep!"

"I'll get up, I tell you."

"Thought thee'd ha' slept through the bed and right through to the floor," said the chambermaid by the door, tittering.

"Unless you pack and go, I'll step out amongst you all!"

Whereat they fled with mock squeals, calling out that the very thought made them blush: and left me to dress.

Downstairs I found a giant's breakfast spread for me, and ate the hole, and felt the better for it: and thereupon paid my scot, resisting the landlady's endeavor to charge me double for the bed, and walked out to see the town.

"Take care o' thysel'," the chambermaid bawled after me; "nor flourish thy attainments abroad, lest they put thee in a show!"

Dark was coming on fast: and to my chagrin (for I had intended purchasing a horse) the buying and selling of the fair were over, the cattle-pens broken up, and the dealers gather'd round the fiddlers, ballad singers, and gingerbread stalls. There were gaming booths, too, driving a brisk trade at Shovel-board, All-fours, and Costly Colors; and an eating tent, whence issued a thick reek of cooking and loud rattle of plates. Over the entrance, I remember, was set a notice: *"Dame Alloway from Bartholomew Fair. Here are the best geese, and she does them as well as ever she did."* I jostled my way along, keeping tight hold on my pockets, for fear of cutpurses; when presently, about halfway down the street, there arose the noise of shouting. The crowd made a rush toward it; and in a minute I was left alone, standing before a juggler who had a sword halfway down his throat, and had to draw it out again before he could with any sufficiency curse the defection of his audience; but offered to pull out a tooth for me if I wanted it.

I left him, and running after the crowd soon learn'd the cause of this tumult.

'Twas a meagre old rascal that someone had charged with picking pockets: and they were dragging him off to be duck'd. Now in the heart of Wantage the little stream that runs through the town is widen'd into a cistern about ten feet square, and five in depth, over which hung a ducking stool for scolding wives. And since the townspeople draw their water from this cistern, 'tis to be supposed they do not fear the infection. A long beam on a pivot hangs out over the pool, and to the end is a chair fasten'd; into which, despite his kicks and screams, they now strapped this poor wretch, whose grey locks might well have won mercy for him.

Souse! he was plunged: hauled up choking and dripping: then—just as he found tongue to shriek—souse! again.

'Twas a dismal punishment; and this time they kept him under for a full half minute. But as the beam was lifted again, I heard a hullaballoo and a cry—

"The bear! the bear!"

And turning, I saw a great brown form lumbering down the street behind, and driving the people before it like chaff.

The crowd at the brink of the pool scatter'd to right and left, yelling. Up flew the beam of the ducking stool, reliev'd of their weight, and down with a splash went the pickpocket at the far end. As well for my own skin's sake as out of pity to see him drowning, I jumped into the water. In two strokes I reach'd him, gained footing, and with Anthony's sword cut the straps away and pull'd him up. And there we stood, up to our necks, coughing and spluttering; while on the deserted brink the bear sniff'd at the water and regarded us.

No doubt we appear'd contemptible enough: for after a time he turned with a louder sniff, and went his way lazily up the street again. He had broken out from the pit wherein, for the best part of the day, they had baited him; yet seemed to bear little malice. For he saunter'd about the town for an hour or two, hurting no man, but making a clean sweep of every sweet stall in his way; and was taken at last very easily, with his head in a treacle cask, by the bear ward and a few dogs.

Meanwhile the pickpocket and I had scrambled out by the further bank and wrung our clothes. He seemed to resent his treatment no more than did the bear.

"Ben cove—'tis a good world. My thanks!"

And with this scant gratitude he was gone, leaving me to make my way back to the sign of "The Boot," where the chambermaid led me upstairs, and took away my clothes to dry by the fire. I determin'd to buy a horse on the morrow, and with my guineas and the King's letter under the pillow, dropp'd off to slumber again.

My powers of sleep must have been nois'd abroad by the hostess: for next morning at the breakfast ordinary, the dealers and drovers laid down knife and fork to stare as I enter'd. After a while one or two lounged out and brought in others to look: so that soon I was in a ring of stupid faces, all gazing like so many cows.

For a while I affected to eat undisturbed: but lost patience at last and addressed a red-headed gazer—

"If you take me for a show, you ought to pay."

"That's fair," said the fellow, and laid a groat on the board. This came near to putting me in a passion, but his face was serious. "'Tis a real pleasure," he added heartily, "to look on one so gifted."

"If any of you," I said, "could sell me a horse—"

At once there was a clamor, all bidding in one breath for my custom. So finishing my breakfast, I walked out with them to the tavern yard, where I had my pick among the sorriest-looking dozen of nags in England, and finally bought from the red-haired man, for five pounds, bridle, saddle, and a flea-bitten grey that seem'd more honestly raw-boned than the rest. And the owner wept tears at the parting with his beast, and thereby added a pang to the fraud he had already put upon me. And I rode from the tavern door suspecting laughter in the eyes of every passer-by.

The day ('twas drawing near noon as I started) was cold and clear, with a coating of rime over the fields: and my horse's feet rang cheerfully on the frozen road. His pace was of the soberest: but, as I was no skilful rider, this suited me rather than not. Only it was galling to be told so, as happened before I had gone three miles.

'Twas my friend the pickpocket: and he sat before a fire of dry sticks a little way back from the road. His scanty hair, stiff as a badger's, now stood upright around his batter'd cap, and he look'd at me over the bushes, with his hook'd nose thrust forward like a bird's beak.

"Bien lightmans, comrade—good day! 'Tis a good world; so stop and dine."

I pull'd up my grey.

"Glad you find it so," I answered; "you had a nigh chance to compare it with the next, last night."

"Shan't do so well i' the next, I fear," he said with a twinkle: "but I owe thee something, and here's a hedgehog that in five minutes'll be baked to a turn. 'Tis a good world, and the better that no man can count on it. Last night my dripping duds helped me to a cant tale, and got me a silver penny from a man of religion. Good's in the worst; and life's like hunting the squirrel—a man gets much good exercise thereat, but seldom what he hunts for."

"That's as good morality as Aristotle's," said I.

"'Tis better for me, because 'tis mine." While I tether'd my horse he blew at the embers, wherein lay a good-sized ball of clay, baking. After a while he look'd up with red cheeks. "They were so fast set on drowning me," he continued with a wink, "they couldn't spare time to look i' my pocket—the ruffin cly them!"

He pull'd the clay ball out of the fire, crack'd it, and lo! inside was a hedgehog cook'd, the spikes sticking in the clay, and coming away with it. So he divided the flesh with his knife, and upon a slice of bread from his wallet it made very delicate eating: tho' I doubt if I enjoyed it as much as did my comrade, who swore over and over that the world was good, and as the wintry sun broke out, and the hot ashes warm'd his knees, began to chatter at a great pace.

"Why, sir, but for the pretty uncertainty of things I'd as lief die here as I sit—"

He broke off at the sound of wheels, and a coach with two postillions spun past us on the road.

I had just time to catch a glimpse of a figure huddled in the corner, and a sweet pretty girl with chestnut curls seated beside it, behind the glass. After the coach came a heavy broad-shoulder'd servant riding on a stout grey; who flung us a sharp glance as he went by, and at twenty yards' distance turn'd again to look.

"That's luck," observed the pickpocket, as the travelers disappear'd down the highway: "Tomorrow, with a slice of it, I might be riding in such a coach as that, and have the hydropsy, to boot. Good lack! when

I was ta'en prisoner by the Turks a-sailing i' the *Mary* of London, and sold for a slave at Algiers, I escap'd, after two months, with Eli Sprat, a Gravesend man, in a small open boat. Well, we sail'd three days and nights, and all the time there was a small sea bird following, flying round and round us, and calling two notes that sounded for all the world like 'Wind'ard! Wind'ard!' So at last says Eli, "'Tis heaven's voice bidding us ply to wind'ard.' And so we did, and on the fourth day made Marseilles; and who should be first to meet Eli on the quay but a Frenchwoman he had married five years before, and left. And the jade had him clapp'd in the pillory, alongside of a cheating fishmonger with a collar of stinking smelts, that turn'd poor Eli's stomach completely. Now there's somewhat to set against the story of Whittington next time 'tis told you."

I was now for bidding the old rascal good-bye. But he offer'd to go with me as far as Hungerford, where we should turn into the Bath road. At first I was shy of accepting, by reason of his coat, wherein patches of blue, orange-tawny and flame-color quite overlaid the parent black: but closed with him upon his promise to teach me the horsemanship that I so sadly lacked. And by time we enter'd Hungerford town I was advanced so far, and bestrode my old grey so easily, that in gratitude I offer'd him supper and bed at an inn, if he would but buy a new coat: to which he agreed, saying that the world was good.

By this, the day was clouded over and the rain coming down apace. So that as soon as my comrade was decently array'd at the first slopshop we came to, 'twas high time to seek an inn. We found quarters at "The Horn," and sought the travelers' room, and a fire to dry ourselves.

In this room, at the window, were two men who look'd lazily up at our entrance. They were playing at a game, which was no other than to race two snails up a pane of glass and wager which should prove the faster.

"A wet day!" said my comrade, cheerfully.

The pair regarded him. "I'll lay you a crown it clears within the hour!" said one.

"And I another," put in the other; and with that they went back to their sport.

Drawing near, I myself was soon as eager as they in watching the snails, when my companion drew my notice to a piece of writing on the window over which they were crawling. 'Twas a set of verses scribbled there, that must have been scratch'd with a diamond: and to my surprise—for I had not guess'd him a scholar—he read them out for my benefit. Thus the writing ran, for I copied it later:

"*Master Ephraim Tucker*, his dying councell to wayfardingers; to seek *The Splendid Spur.*

"Not on the necks of prince or hound,
  Nor on a woman's finger twin'd,
May gold from the deriding ground
  Keep sacred that we sacred bind
    Only the heel
    Of splendid steel
Shall stand secure on sliding fate,
When golden navies weep their freight.

"The scarlet hat, the laurell'd stave
  Are measures, not the springs, of worth;
In a wife's lap, as in a grave,
  Man's airy notions mix with earth.
    Seek other spur
    Bravely to stir
The dust in this loud world, and tread
Alp-high among the whisp'ring dead.

"Trust in thyself,—then spur amain:
  So shall Charybdis wear a grace,
Grim Aetna laugh, the Lybian plain

Take roses to her shrivell'd face.
This orb—this round
Of sight and sound—
Count it the lists that God hath built
For haughty hearts to ride a-tilt.

"FINIS-Master Tucker's Farewell."

"And a very pretty moral on four gentlemen that pass their afternoon a setting snails to race!"

At these words, spoken in a delicate foreign voice we all started round: and saw a young lady standing behind us.

Now that she was the one who had passed us in the coach I saw at once. But describe her—to be plain—I cannot, having tried a many times. So let me say only that she was the prettiest creature on God's earth (which, I hope, will satisfy her); that she had chestnut curls and a mouth made for laughing; that she wore a kirtle and bodice of grey silk taffety, with a gold pomander-box hung on a chain about her neck; and held out a drinking glass toward us with a Frenchified grace.

"Gentlemen, my father is sick, and will taste no water but what is freshly drawn. I ask you not to brave Charybdis or Aetna, but to step out into the rainy yard and draw me a glassful from the pump there: for our servant is abroad in the town."

To my deep disgust, before I could find a word, that villainous old pickpocket had caught the glass from her hand and reached the door. But I ran after; and out into the yard we stepp'd together, where I pump'd while he held the glass to the spout, flinging away the contents time after time, till the bubbles on the brim, and the film on the outside, were to his liking.

'Twas he, too, that gain'd the thanks on our return.

"Mistress," said he with a bow, "my young friend is raw, but has a good will. Confess, now, for his edification—for he is bound on a long journey westward, where, they tell me, the maidens grow comeliest—that looks avail naught with womankind beside a dashing manner."

The young gentlewoman laughed, shaking her curls.

"I'll give him in that case three better counsels yet: first (for by his habit I see he is on the King's side), let him take a circuit from this place to the south, for the road between Marlboro' and Bristol is, they tell me, all held by the rebels; next, let him avoid all women, even tho' they ask but an innocent cup of water; and lastly, let him shun thee, unless thy face lie more than thy tongue. Shall I say more?"

"Why, no—perhaps better not," replied the old rogue hastily, but laughing all the same. "That's a clever lass," he added, as the door shut behind her.

And, indeed, I was fain, next morning, to agree to this. For, awaking, I found my friend (who had shar'd a room with me) already up and gone, and discovered the reason in a sheet of writing pinn'd to my clothes—

"Young Sir,—I convict myself of ingratitude: but habit is hard to break. So I have made off with the half of thy guineas and thy horse. The residue, and the letter thou bearest, I leave. 'Tis a good world, and experience should be bought early. This golden lesson I leave in return for the guineas. Believe me, 'tis of more worth. Read over those verses on the windowpane before starting, digest them, and trust me, thy obliged,

"Peter, The Jackman.

"Raise not thy hand so often to thy breast: 'tis a sure index of hidden valuables."

Be sure I was wroth enough: nor did the calm interest of the two snail owners appease me, when at breakfast I told them a part of the story. But I thought I read sympathy in the low price at which one of them offer'd me his horse. 'Twas a tall black brute, very strong in the loins, and I bought him at once out of my shrunken stock of guineas. At ten o'clock, I set out, not along the Bath road, but bearing to the south, as the young gentlewoman had counselled. I began to hold a high opinion of her advice.

By twelve o'clock I was back at the inn door, clamoring to see the man that sold me the horse, which had gone dead lame after the second mile.

"Dear heart!" cried the landlord; "they are gone, the both, this hour and a half. But they are coming again within the fortnight; and I'm expressly to report if you return'd, as they had a wager about it."

I turn'd away, pondering. Two days on the road had put me sadly out of conceit with myself. For mile upon mile I trudged, dragging the horse after me by the bridle, till my arms felt as if coming from their sockets. I would have turn'd the brute loose, and thought myself well quit of him, had it not been for the saddle and bridle he carried.

* * * * *

'Twas about five in the evening, and I still laboring along, when, over the low hedge to my right, a man on a sorrel mare leap'd easily as a swallow, and alighted some ten paces or less in front of me; where he dismounted and stood barring my path. The muzzle of his pistol was in my face before I could lay hand to my own.

"Good evening!" said I.

"You have money about you, doubtless," growled the man curtly, and in a voice that made me start. For by his voice and figure in the dusk I knew him for Captain Settle: and in the sorrel with the high white stocking I recognized the mare, Molly, that poor Anthony Killigrew had given me almost with his last breath.

The bully did not know me, having but seen me for an instant at "The Crown," and then in very different attire.

"I have but a few poor coins," I answer'd.

"Then hand 'em over."

"Be shot if I do!" said I in a passion; and pulling out a handful from my pocket, I dash'd them down in the road.

For a moment the Captain took his pistol from my face, and stooped to clutch at the golden coins as they trickled and ran to right and left. The next, I had struck out with my right fist, and down he went staggering. His pistol dropped out of his hand and exploded between my feet. I rush'd to Molly, caught her bridle, and leap'd on her back. 'Twas a near thing, for the Captain was rushing toward us. But at the call of my voice the mare gave a bound and turn'd: and down the road I was borne, light as a feather.

A bullet whizz'd past my ear: I heard the Captain's curse mingle with the report: and then was out of range, and galloping through the dusk.

CHAPTER V.

MY ADVENTURE AT THE "THREE CUPS."

Secure of pursuit, and full of delight in the mare's easy motion, I must have travelled a good six miles before the moon rose. In the frosty sky her rays sparkled cheerfully, and by them I saw on the holsters the silver demi-bear that I knew to be the crest of the Killigrews, having the fellow to it engraved on my sword-hilt. So now I was certain 'twas Molly that I bestrode: and took occasion of the light to explore the holsters and saddle flap.

Poor Anthony's pistols were gone—filched, no doubt, by the Captain: but you may guess my satisfaction, when on thrusting my hand deeper, I touched a heap of coins, and found them to be gold.

'Twas certainly a rare bargain I had driven with Captain Settle. For the five or six gold pieces I scatter'd on the road, I had won close on thirty guineas, as I counted in the moonlight; not to speak of this incomparable Molly. And I began to whistle gleefully, and taste the joke over again and laugh to myself, as we cantered along with the north wind at our backs.

All the same, I had no relish for riding thus till morning. For the night was chill enough to search my very bones after the heat of the late gallop: and, moreover, I knew nothing of the road, which at this hour was quite deserted. So that, coming at length to a tall hill with a black ridge of pine wood standing up against the moon like a fish's fin, I was glad enough to note below it, and at some distance from the trees, a window brightly lit; and pushed forward in hope of entertainment.

The building was an inn, though a sorry one. Nor, save for the lighted window, did it wear any grace of hospitality, but thrust out a bare shoulder upon the road, and a sign that creaked overhead and look'd for all the world like a gallows. Round this shoulder of the house, and into the main yard (that turn'd churlishly toward the hillside), the wind howled like a beast in pain. I climb'd off Molly, and pressing my hat down on my head, struck a loud rat-tat on the door.

Curiously, it opened at once; and I saw a couple of men in the lighted passage.

"Heard the mare's heels on the road, Cap—. Hillo! What in the fiend's name is this?"

Said I: "If you are he that keeps this house, I want two things of you—first, a civil tongue, and next a bed."

"Ye'll get neither, then."

"Your sign says that you keep an inn."

"Aye—the 'Three Cups': but we're full."

"Your manner of speech proves that to be a lie."

I liked the fellow's voice so little that 'tis odds I would have re-mounted Molly and ridden away; but at this instant there floated down the stairs and out through the drink-smelling passage a sound that made me jump. 'Twas a girl's voice singing—

"Hey nonni—nonni—no!
Men are fools that wish to die!
Is't not fine to laugh and sing
When the hells of death do ring—"

There was no doubt upon it. The voice belonged to the young gentlewoman I had met at Hungerford. I turned sharply toward the landlord, and was met by another surprise. The second man, that till now had stood well back in the shadow, was peering forward, and devouring Molly with his gaze. 'Twas hard to read his features, but then and there I would have wagered my life he was no other than Luke Settle's comrade, Black Dick.

My mind was made up. "I'll not ride a step further, to-night," said I.

"Then bide there and freeze," answer'd the landlord.

He was for slamming the door in my face, when the other caught him by the arm and, pulling him a little back, whisper'd a word or two. I guess'd what this meant, but resolved not to draw back; and presently the landlord's voice began again, betwixt surly and polite—

"Have ye too high a stomach to lie on straw?"

"Oho!" thought I to myself, "then I am to be kept for the mare's sake, but not admitted to the house:" and said aloud that I could put up with a straw bed.

"Because there's the stable loft at your service. As ye hear" (and in fact the singing still went on, only now I heard a man's voice joining in the catch) "our house is full of company. But straw is clean bedding, and the mare I'll help to put in stall."

"Agreed," I said, "on one condition—that you send out a maid to me with a cup of mulled sack: for this cold eats me alive."

To this he consented: and stepping back into a side room with the other fellow, returned in a minute alone, and carrying a lantern which, in spite of the moon, was needed to guide a stranger across that ruinous yard. The flare, as we pick'd our way along, fell for a moment on an open cart shed and, within, on the gilt panels of a coach that I recogniz'd. In the stable, that stood at the far end of the court, I was surprised to find half a dozen horses standing, ready saddled, and munching their fill of oats. They were ungroom'd, and one or two in a lather of sweat that on such a night was hard to account for. But I asked no questions, and my companion vouchsafed no talk, though twice I caught him regarding me curiously as I unbridled the mare in the only vacant stall. Not a word pass'd as he took the lantern off the peg again, and led the way up a ramshackle ladder to the loft above. He was a fat, lumbering fellow, and made the old timbers creak. At the top he set down the light, and pointed to a heap of straw in the corner.

"Yon's your bed," he growled; and before I could answer, was picking his way down the ladder again.

I look'd about, and shiver'd. The eaves of my bedchamber were scarce on speaking terms with the walls, and through a score of crannies at least the wind poured and whistled, so that after shifting my truss of straw a dozen times I found myself still the centre of a whirl of draught. The candle-flame, too, was puffed this way and that inside the horn sheath. I was losing patience when I heard footsteps below; the ladder creak'd, and the red hair and broad shoulders of a chambermaid rose into view. She carried a steaming mug in her hand, and mutter'd all the while in no very choice talk.

The wench had a kind face, tho'; and a pair of eyes that did her more credit than her tongue.

"And what's to be my reward for this, I want to know?" she panted out, resting her left palm on her hip.

"Why, a groat or two," said I, "when it comes to the reckoning."

"Lud!" she cried, "what a dull young man!"

"Dull?"

"Aye—to make me ask for a kiss in so many words:" and with the back of her left hand she wiped her mouth for it frankly, while she held out the mug in her right.

"Oh!" I said, "I beg your pardon, but my wits are frozen up, I think. There's two, for interest: and another if you tell me whom your master entertains to-night, that I must be content with this crib."

She took the kisses with composure and said—

"Well—to begin, there's the gentlefolk that came this afternoon with their own carriage and heathenish French servant: a cranky old grandee and a daughter with more airs than a peacock: Sir Something-or-other Killigew—Lord bless the boy!"

For I had dropp'd the mug and split the hot sack all about the straw, where it trickled away with a fragrance reproachfully delicious.

"Now I beg your pardon a hundred times: but the chill is in my bones worse than the ague;" and huddling my shoulders up, I counterfeited a shivering fit with a truthfulness that surpris'd myself.

"Poor lad!"

"—And 'tis first hot and then cold all down my spine."

"There, now!"

"-And goose flesh and flushes all over my body."

"Dear heart-and to pass the night in this grave of a place!"

"—And by morning I shall be in a high fever: and oh! I feel I shall die of it!"

"Don't—don't!" The honest girl's eyes were full of tears. "I wonder, now—" she began: and I waited, eager for her next words. "Sure, master's at cards in the parlor, and 'll be drunk by midnight. Shalt pass the night by the kitchen fire, if only thou make no noise."

"But your mistress—what will she say?"

"Is in heaven these two years: and out of master's speaking distance forever. So blow out the light and follow me gently."

Still feigning to shiver, I follow'd her down the ladder, and through the stable into the open. The wind by this time had brought up some heavy clouds, and mass'd them about the moon: but 'twas freezing hard, nevertheless. The girl took me by the hand to guide me: for, save from the one bright window in the upper floor, there was no light at all in the yard. Clearly, she was in dread of her master's anger, for we stole across like ghosts, and once or twice she whisper'd a warning when my toe kick'd against a loose cobble. But just as I seem'd to be walking into a stone wall, she put out her hand, I heard the click of a latch, and stood in a dark, narrow passage.

The passage led to a second door that open'd on a wide, stone-pav'd kitchen, lit by a cheerful fire, whereon a kettle hissed and bubbled as the vapor lifted the cover. Close by the chimney corner was a sort of trap, or buttery hatch, for pushing the hot dishes conveniently into the parlor on the other side of the wall. Besides this, for furniture, the room held a broad deal table, an oak dresser, a linen press, a rack with hams and strings of onions depending from it, a settle and a chair or two, with (for decoration) a dozen or so of ballad sheets stuck among the dish covers along the wall.

"Sit," whisper'd the girl, "and make no noise, while I brew a rack-punch for the men-folk in the parlor." She jerked her thumb toward the buttery hatch, where I had already caught the mur-mer of voices.

I took up a chair softly, and set it down between the hatch and the fireplace, so that while warming my knees I could catch any word spoken more than ordinary loud on the other side of the wall. The chambermaid stirr'd the fire briskly, and moved about singing as she fetch'd down bottles and glasses from the dresser—

> "Lament ye maids an' darters
>   For constant Sarah Ann,
> Who hang'd hersel' in her garters
>   All for the love o' man,
> All for the—"

She was pausing, bottle in hand, to take the high note: but hush'd suddenly at the sound of the voices singing in the room upstairs—

> "Vivre en tout cas
> C'est le grand soulas
> Des honnetes gens!"

"That's the foreigners," said the chambermaid, and went on with her ditty—

> "All for the love of a souljer
> Who christening name was Jan."

A volley of oaths sounded through the buttery hatch.

"—And that's the true-born Englishmen, as you may tell by their speech. 'Tis pretty company the master keeps, these days."

She was continuing her song, when I held up a finger for silence. In fact, through the hatch my ear had caught a sentence that set me listening for more with a still heart.

"D—n the Captain," the landlord's gruff voice was saying; "I warn'd 'n agen this fancy business when sober, cool-handed work was toward."

"Settle's way from his cradle," growl'd another; "and times enough I've told 'n: 'Cap'n,' says I, 'there's no sense o' proportions about ye.' A master mind, sirs, but 'a 'll be hang'd for a hen-roost, so sure as my name's Bill Widdicomb."

"Ugly words-what a creeping influence has that same mention o' hanging!" piped a thinner voice.

"Hold thy complaints, Old Mortification," put in a speaker that I recogniz'd for Black Dick; "sure the pretty maid upstairs is tender game. Hark how they sing!"

And indeed the threatened folk upstairs were singing their catch very choicely, with a girl's clear voice to lead them—

"Comment dit papa
—Margoton, ma mie?"

"Heathen language, to be sure," said the thin voice again, as the chorus ceased: "thinks I to mysel' 'they be but Papisters,' an' my doubting mind is mightily reconcil'd to manslaughter."

"I don't like beginning 'ithout the Cap'n," observed Black Dick: "though I doubt something has miscarried. Else, how did that young spark ride in upon the mare?"

"An' that's what thy question should ha' been, Dick, with a pistol to his skull."

"He'll keep till the morrow."

"We'll give Settle half-an-hour more," said the landlord: "Mary!" he push'd open the hatch, so that I had barely time to duck my head out of view, "fetch in the punch, girl. How did'st leave the young man i' the loft?'

"Asleep, or nearly," answer'd Mary—

> "Who hang'd hersel' in her gar-ters,
> All for the love o' man—"

"—Anon, anon, master: wait only till I get the kettle on the boil."

The hatch was slipp'd to again. I stood up and made a step toward the girl.

"How many are they?" I ask'd, jerking a finger in the direction of the parlor.

"A dozen all but one."

"Where is the foreign guests' room?"

"Left hand, on the first landing."

"The staircase?"

"Just outside the door."

"Then sing—go on singing for your life."

"But—"

"Sing!"

"Dear heart, they'll murder thee! Oh! for pity's sake, let go my wrist—

> "'Lament, ye maids an' darters—'"

I stole to the door and peep'd out. A lantern hung in the passage, and showed the staircase directly in front of me. I stay'd for a moment to pull off my boots, and, holding them in my left hand, crept up the stairs. In the kitchen, the girl was singing and clattering the glasses together. Behind the door, at the head of the stairs, I heard voices talking. I slipp'd on my boots again and tapp'd on the panel.

"Come in!"

Let me try to describe that on which my eyes rested as I push'd the door wide. 'Twas a long room, wainscoted half up the wall in some dark wood, and in daytime lit by one window only, which now was hung with red curtains. By the fireplace, where a brisk wood fire was crackling, lean'd the young gentlewoman I had met at Hungerford, who, as she now turn'd her eyes upon me, ceas'd fingering the guitar or mandoline that she held against her waist, and raised her pretty head not without curiosity.

But 'twas on the table in the centre of the chamber that my gaze settled; and on two men beside it, of whom I must speak more particularly.

The elder, who sat in a high-back'd chair, was a little, frail, deform'd gentleman of about fifty, dress'd very richly in dark velvet and furs, and wore on his head a velvet skullcap, round which his white hair stuck up like a ferret's. But the oddest thing about him was a complexion that any maid of sixteen would give her ears for—of a pink and white so transparent that it seem'd a soft light must be glowing beneath his skin. On either cheek bone this delicate coloring centred in a deeper flush. This is as much as I need say about his appearance, except that his eyes were very bright and sharp, and his chin stuck out like a vicious mule's.

The table before him was cover'd with bottles and flasks, in the middle of which stood a silver lamp burning, and over it a silver saucepan that sent up a rare fragrance as the liquid within it simmer'd and bubbled. So eager was the old gentleman in watching the progress of his mixture, that he merely glanc'd up at my entrance, and then, holding up a hand for silence, turn'd his eyes on the saucepan again.

The second man was the broad-shouldered lackey I had seen riding behind the coach: and now stood over the saucepan with a twisted flask in his hand, from which he pour'd a red syrup very gingerly, drop by drop, with the tail of his eye turn'd on his master's face, that he might know when to cease.

Now it may be that my entrance upset this experiment in strong drinks. At any rate, I had scarce come to a stand about three paces inside the door, when the little old gentleman bounces up in a fury, kicks over his chair, hurls the nearest bottles to right and left, and sends the silver saucepan spinning across the table to my very feet, where it scalded me clean through the boot, and made me hop for pain.

"Spoil'd—spoil'd!" he scream'd: "drench'd in filthy liquor, when it should have breath'd but a taste!"

And, to my amazement, he sprang on the strapping servant like a wild-cat, and began to beat, cuff, and belabor him with all the strength of his puny limbs.

'Twas like a scene out of Bedlam. Yet all the while the girl lean'd quietly against the mantelshelf, and softly touched the strings of her instrument; while the servant took the rain of blows and slaps as though 'twere a summer shower, grinning all over his face, and making no resistance at all.

Then, as I stood dumb with perplexity, the old gentleman let go his hold of the fellow's hair, and, dropping on the floor, began to roll about in a fit of coughing, the like of which no man can imagine. 'Twas hideous. He bark'd, and writhed, and bark'd again, till the disorder seem'd to search and rack every innermost inch of his small frame. And in the intervals of coughing his exclamations were terrible to listen to.

"He's dying!" I cried; and ran forward to help.

The servant pick'd up the chair, and together we set him in it. By degrees the violence of the cough abated, and he lay back, livid in the face, with his eyes closed, and his hands clutching the knobs of the chair. I turn'd to the girl. She had neither spoken nor stirr'd, but now came forward, and calmly ask'd my business.

"I think," said I, "that your name is Killigrew?"

"I am Delia Killigrew, and this is my father, Sir Deakin."

"Now on his way to visit his estates in Cornwall?"

She nodded.

"Then I have to warn you that your lives are in danger." And, gently as possible, I told her what I had seen and heard downstairs. In the middle of my tale, the servant stepp'd to the door, and return'd quietly. There was no lock on the inside. After a minute he went across, and drew the red curtains. The window had a grating within, of iron bars as thick as a man's thumb, strongly clamp'd in the stonework, and not four inches apart. Clearly, he was a man of few words; for, returning, he merely pull'd out his sword, and waited for the end of my tale.

The girl, also, did not interrupt me, but listen'd in silence. As I ceas'd, she said—

"Is this all you know?"

"No," answer'd I, "it is not. But the rest I promise to tell you if we escape from this place alive. Will this content you?"

She turn'd to the servant, who nodded. Whereupon she held out her hand very cordially.

"Sir, listen: we are travelers bound for Cornwall, as you know, and have some small possessions, that will poorly reward the greed of these violent men. Nevertheless, we should be hurrying on our journey did we not await my brother Anthony, who was to have ridden from Oxford to join us here, but has been delayed, doubtless on the King's business—"

She broke off, as I started: for below I heard the main door open, and Captain Settle's voice in the passage. The arch villain had return'd.

"Mistress Delia," I said hurriedly, "the twelfth man has enter'd the house, and unless we consider our plans at once, all's up with us."

"Tush!" said the old gentleman in the chair, who (it seems) had heard all, and now sat up brisk as ever. "I, for my part shall mix another glass, and leave it all to Jacques. Come, sit by me, sir, and you shall see some pretty play. Why, Jacques is the neatest rogue with a small sword in all France!"

"Sir," I put in, "they are a round dozen in all, and your life at present is not worth a penny's purchase."

"That's a lie! 'Tis worth this bowl before me, that, with or without you, I mean to empty. What a fool thing is youth! Sir, you must be a dying man like myself to taste life properly." And, as I am a truthful man, he struck up quavering merrily—

"Hey, nonni—nonni—no!
Men are fools that wish to die!
Is't not fine to laugh and sing
When the bells of death do ring?
Is't not fine to drown in wine,
And turn upon the toe,
And sing, hey—nonni—no?
Hey, nonni—nonni—"

"—Come and sit, sir, nor spoil sport. You are too raw, I'll wager, to be of any help; and boggling I detest."

"Indeed, sir," I broke in, now thoroughly anger'd, "I can use the small sword as well as another."

"Tush! Try him, Jacques."

Jacques, still wearing a stolid face, brought his weapon to the guard. Stung to the quick, I wheel'd round, and made a lunge or two, that he put aside as easily as though I were a babe. And then—I know not how it happened, but my sword slipp'd like ice out of my grasp, and went flying across the room. Jacques, sedately as on a matter of business, stepp'd to pick it up, while the old gentleman chuckled.

I was hot and asham'd, and a score of bitter words sprang to my tongue-tip, when the Frenchman, as he rose from stooping, caught my eye, and beckon'd me across to him.

He was white as death, and pointed to the hilt of my sword and the demi-bear engrav'd thereon.

"He is dead," I whisper'd: "hush!—turn your face aside—killed by those same dogs that are now below."

I heard a sob in the true fellow's throat. But on the instant it was drown'd by the sound of a door opening and the tramp of feet on the stairs.

CHAPTER VI.

THE FLIGHT IN THE PINE WOOD.

By the sound of their steps I guess'd one or two of these dozen rascals to be pretty far gone in drink, and afterward found this to be the case. I look'd round. Sir Deakin had pick'd up the lamp and was mixing his bowl of punch, humming to himself without the least concern—

> "Vivre en tout cas
> C'est le grand soulas"—

with a glance at his daughter's face, that was white to the lips, but firmly set.

"Hand me the nutmeg yonder," he said, and then, "why, daughter, what's this?—a trembling hand?"

And all the while the footsteps were coming up.

There was a loud knock on the door.

"Come in!" call'd Sir Deakin.

At this, Jacques, who stood ready for battle by the entrance, wheeled round, shot a look at his master, and dropping his point, made a sign to me to do the same. The door was thrust rudely open, and Captain Settle, his hat cock'd over one eye, and sham drunkenness in his gait, lurched into the room, with the whole villainous crew behind him, huddled on the threshold. Jacques and I stepp'd quietly back, so as to cover the girl.

"Would you mind waiting a moment?" inquir'd Sir Deakin, without looking up, but rubbing the nutmeg calmly up and down the grater: "a fraction too much, and the whole punch will be spoil'd."

It took the Captain aback, and he came to a stand, eyeing us, who look'd back at him without saying a word. And this discomposed him still further.

There was a minute during which the two parties could hear each other's breathing. Sir Deakin set down the nutmeg, wiped his thin white fingers on a napkin, and address'd the Captain sweetly—

"Before asking your business, sir, I would beg you and your company to taste this liquor, which, in the court of France"—the old gentleman took a sip from the mixing ladle—"has had the extreme honor to be pronounced divine." He smack'd his lips, and rising to his feet, let his right hand rest on the silver foot of the lamp as he bowed to the Captain.

Captain Settle's bravado was plainly oozing away before this polite audacity: and seeing Sir Deakin taste the punch, he pull'd off his cap in a shamefaced manner and sat down by the table with a word of thanks.

"Come in, sirs—come in!" call'd the old gentleman; "and follow your friend's example. 'Twill be a compliment to make me mix another bowl when this is finish'd." He stepped around the table to welcome them, still resting his hand on the lamp, as if for steadiness. I saw his eye twinkle as they shuffled in and stood around the chair where the Captain was seated.

"Jacques, bring glasses from the cupboard yonder! And, Delia, fetch up some chairs for our guests—no, sirs, pray do not move!"

He had waved his hand lightly to the door as he turned to us: and in an instant the intention as well as the bright success of this comedy flash'd upon me. There was now no one between us and the stairs, and as for Sir Deakin himself, he had already taken the step of putting the table's width between him and his guests.

I touch'd the girl's arm, and we made as if to fetch a couple of chairs that stood against the wainscot by the door. As we did so, Sir Deakin push'd the punch bowl forward under the Captain's nose.

"Smell, sir," he cried airily, "and report to your friends on the foretaste."

Settle's nose hung over the steaming compound. With a swift pass of the hand, the old gentleman caught up the lamp and had shaken a drop of burning oil into the bowl. A great blaze leap'd to the ceiling. There was a howl—a scream of pain; and as I push'd Mistress Delia through the doorway and out to the head of the stairs, I caught a backward glimpse of Sir Deakin rushing after us, with one of the stoutest among the robbers at his heels.

"Downstairs, for your life!" I whisper'd to the girl, and turning, as her father tumbled past me, let his pursuer run on my sword, as on a spit. At the same instant, another blade pass'd through the fellow transversely, and Jacques stood beside me, with his back to the lintel.

As we pull'd our swords out and the man dropp'd, I had a brief view into the room, where now the blazing liquid ran off the table in a stream. Settle, stamping with agony, had his palms press'd against his scorch'd eyelids. The fat landlord, in trying to beat out the flames, had increased them by upsetting two bottles of aqua vitae, and was dancing about with three fingers in his mouth. The rest stood for the most part dumbfounder'd: but Black Dick had his pistol lifted.

Jacques and I sprang out for the landing and round the doorway. Between the flash and the report I felt a sudden scrape, as of a red-hot wire, across my left thigh and just above the knee.

"Tenez, camarade," said Jacques' voice in my ear; "a moi la porte—a vous le maitre, la-bas:" and he pointed down the staircase, where, by the glare of the conflagration that beat past us, I saw the figures of Sir Deakin and his daughter standing.

"But how can you keep the door against a dozen?"

The Frenchman shrugg'd his shoulders with a smile—

"Mais-comme ca!"

For at this moment came a rush of footsteps within the room. I saw a fat paunch thrusting past us, a quiet pass of steel, and the landlord was wallowing on his face across the threshold. Jacques' teeth snapp'd together as he stood ready for another victim: and as the fellows within the room tumbled back, he motion'd me to leave him.

I sprang from his side, and catching the rail of the staircase, reach'd the foot in a couple of bounds.

"Hurry!" I cried, and caught the old baronet by the hand. His daughter took the other, and between us we hurried him across the passage for the kitchen door.

Within, the chambermaid was on her knees by the settle, her face and apron of the same hue. I saw she was incapable of helping, and hasten'd across the stone floor, and out toward the back entrance.

A stream of icy wind blew in our faces as we stepp'd over the threshold. The girl and I bent our heads to it, and stumbling, tripping, and panting, pull'd Sir Deakin with us out into the cold air.

The yard was no longer dark. In the room above someone had push'd the casement open, letting in the wind: and by this 'twas very evident the room was on fire. Indeed, the curtains had caught, and as we ran, a pennon of flame shot out over our heads, licking the thatch. In the glare of it the outbuildings and the yard gate stood clearly out from the night. I heard the trampling of feet, the sound of Settle's voice shouting an order, and then a dismal yell and clash of steel as we flung open the gate.

"Jacques!" scream'd the old gentleman: "my poor Jacques! Those dogs will mangle him with their cut and thrust—"

'Twas very singular and sad, but as if in answer to Sir Deakin's cry, we heard the brave fellow's voice; and a famous shout it must have been to reach us over the roaring of the flames—

"Mon maitre-mon maitre!" he call'd twice, and then "Sauve toi!" in a fainter voice, yet clear. And after that only a racket of shouts and outcries reach'd us. Without doubt the villains had overpower'd and slain this brave servant. In spite of our peril (for they would be after us at once),'twas all we could do to drag the old man from the gate and up the road: and as he went he wept like a child.

After about fifty yards, we turn'd in at a gate, and began to cut across a field: for I hop'd thus not only to baffle pursuit for a while, but also to gain the wood that we saw dimly ahead. It reach'd to the top of the hill, and I knew not how far beyond: and as I was reflecting that there lay our chance of safety, I heard the inn door below burst open with loud cries, and the sound of footsteps running up the road after us.

Moreover, to complete our fix, the clouds that had been scurrying across the moon's face, now for a minute left a clear interval of sky about her: so that right in our course there lay a great patch brilliantly lit, whereon our figures could be spied at once by anyone glancing into the field. Also, it grew evident that Sir Deakin's late agility was but a short and sudden triumph of will over body: for his poor crooked legs began to trail and lag sadly. So turning sharp about, we struck for the hedge's shadow, and there pull'd him down in a dry ditch, and lay with a hand on his mouth to stifle his ejaculations, while we ourselves held our breathing.

The runners came up the road, pausing for a moment by the gate. I heard it creak, and saw two or three dark forms enter the field—the remainder tearing on up the road with a great clatter of boots.

"Alas, my poor Jacques!" moan'd Sir Deakin: "and to be butcher'd so, that never in his days kill'd a man but as if he lov'd him!"

"Sir," I whisper'd harshly, "if you keep this noise I must gag you." And with that he was silent for awhile.

There was a thick tangle of brambles in the ditch where we lay: and to this we owe our lives. For one of the men, coming our way, pass'd within two yards of us, with the flat of his sword beating the growth over our heads.

"Reu-ben! Reuben Gedges!" call'd a voice by the gate.

The fellow turn'd; and peeping between the bramble twigs, I saw the moonlight glittering on his blade. A narrow, light-hair'd man he was, with a weak chin: and since then I have paid him out for the fright he gave us.

"What's the coil?" he shouted back.

"The stable roofs ablaze—for the Lord's sake come and save the hosses!"

He strode back, and in a minute the field was clear. Creeping out with caution, I grew aware of two mournful facts: first, that the stable was indeed afire, as I perceiv'd by standing on tiptoe and looking over the hedge; and second, that my knee was hurt by Black Dick's bullet. The muscles had stiffened while we were crouching, and now pain'd me badly. Yet I kept it to myself as we started off again to run.

But at the stile that, at the top of the field, led into the woods, I pull'd up—

"Sorry I am to say it, but you must go on without me."

"O—oh!" cried the girl.

"'Tis for your safety. See, I leave a trail of blood behind me, so that when day rises they will track us easily."

And sure enough, even by the moon, 'twas easy to trace the dark spots on the grass and earth beside the stile. My left boot, too, was full of blood.

She was silent for awhile. Down in the valley we could hear the screams of the poor horses. The light of the flames lit up the pine trunks about us to a bright scarlet.

"Sir, you hold our gratitude cheaply."

She unwound the kerchief from her neck, and making me sit on the stile, bound up my knee skillfully, twisting a short stick in the bandage to stop the bleeding.

I thank'd her, and we hurried on into the depths of the wood, treading silently on the deep carpet of pine needles. The ground rose steeply all the way: and all the way, tho' the light grew feebler, the roar and outcries in the valley follow'd us.

Toward the hill's summit the trees were sparser. Looking upward, I saw that the sky had grown thickly overcast. We cross'd the ridge, and after a minute or so were in thick cover again.

'Twas here that Sir Deakin's strength gave out. Almost without warning, he sank down between our hands, and in a second was taken with that hateful cough, that once already this night had frightened me for his life.

"Ah, ah!" he groaned, between the spasms, "I'm not fit—I'm not fit for it!" and was taken again, and roll'd about barking, so that I fear'd the sound would bring all Settle's gang on our heels. "I'm not fit for it!" he repeated, as the cough left him, and he lay back helpless, among the pine needles.

Now, I understood his words to bear on his unfitness for death, and judg'd them very decent and properly spoken: and took occasion to hint this in my attempts to console him.

"Why, bless the boy!" he cried, sitting up and staring, "for what d'ye think I'm unsuited?"

"Why, to die, sir—to be sure!"

"Holy Mother!" he regarded me with surprise, contempt and pity, all together: "was ever such a dunderhead! If ever man were fit to die, I am he—and that's just my reasonable complaint. Heart alive! 'tis unfit to *live* I am, tied to this absurd body!"

I suppose my attitude express'd my lack of comprehension, for he lifted a finger and went on—

"Tell me—can you eat beef, and drink beer, and enjoy them?"

"Why, yes."

"And fight—hey? and kiss a pretty girl, and be glad you've done it? Dear, dear, how I do hate a fool and a fool's pity! Lift me up and carry me a step. This night's work has kill'd me: I feel it in my lungs. 'Tis a pity, too; for I was just beginning to enjoy it."

74

I lifted him as I would a babe, and off we set again, my teeth shutting tight on the pain of my hurt. And presently, coming to a little dingle, about half a mile down the hillside, well hid with dead bracken and blackberry bushes, I consulted with the girl. The place was well shelter'd from the wind that rock'd the treetops, and I fear'd to go much further, for we might come on open country at any moment and so double our peril. It seem'd best, therefore, to lay the old gentleman snugly in the bottom of this dingle and wait for day. And with my buff-coat, and a heap of dried leaves, I made him fairly easy, reserving my cloak to wrap about Mistress Delia's fair neck and shoulders. But against this at first she protested.

"For how are you to manage?" she ask'd.

"I shall tramp up and down, and keep watch," answer'd I, strewing a couch for her beside her father: "and 'tis but fair exchange for the kerchief you gave me from your own throat."

At last I persuaded her, and she crept close to her father, and under the edge of the buff-coat for warmth. There was abundance of dry bracken in the dingle, and with this and some handfuls of pine needles, I cover'd them over, and left them to find what sleep they might.

For two hours and more after this, I hobbled to and fro near them, as well as my wound would allow, looking up at the sky through the pine tops, and listening to the sobbing of the wind. Now and then I would swing my arms for warmth, and breathe on my fingers, that were sorely benumb'd; and all the while kept my ears on the alert, but heard nothing.

'Twas, as I said, something over two hours after, that I felt a soft cold touch, and then another, like kisses on my forehead. I put up my hand, and looked up again at the sky. As I did so, the girl gave a long sigh, and awoke from her doze—

"Sure, I must have dropp'd asleep," she said, opening her eyes, and spying my shadow above her: "has aught happened?"

"Aye," replied I, "something is happening that will wipe out our traces and my bloody track."

"And what is that?"

"Snow: see, 'tis falling fast."

She bent over, and listen'd to her father's breathing.

"'Twill kill him," she said simply.

I pull'd some more fronds of the bracken to cover them both. She thank'd me, and offer'd to relieve me in my watch: which I refus'd. And indeed, by lying down I should have caught my death, very likely.

The big flakes drifted down between the pines: till, as the moon paled, the ground about me was carpeted all in white, with the foliage black as ink above it. Time after time, as I tramp'd to and fro, I paus'd to brush the fresh-forming heap from the sleepers' coverlet, and shake it gently from the tresses of the girl's hair. The old man's face was covered completely by the buff-coat: but his breathing was calm and regular as any child's.

Day dawn'd. Awaking Mistress Delia, I ask'd her to keep watch for a time, while I went off to explore. She crept out from her bed with a little shiver of disgust.

"Run about," I advis'd, "and keep the blood stirring."

She nodded: and looking back, as I strode down the hill, I saw her moving about quickly, swinging her arms, and only pausing to wave a hand to me for goodspeed.

* * * * *

'Twas an hour before I return'd: and plenty I had to tell. Only at the entrance to the dingle the words failed from off my tongue. The old gentleman lay as he had lain throughout the night. But the bracken had been toss'd aside, and the girl was kneeling over him. I drew near, my step not arousing her. Sir Deakin's face was pale and calm: but on the snow that had gather'd by his head, lay a red streak of blood. 'Twas from his lungs, and he was quite dead.

CHAPTER VII.

I FIND A COMRADE.

But I must go back a little and tell you what befell in my expedition.

I had scarce trudged out of sight of my friends, down the hill, when it struck me that my footprints in the snow were in the last degree dangerous to them, and might lead Settle and his crew straight to the dingle. Here was a fix. I stood for some minutes nonpluss'd, when above the stillness of the wood (for the wind had dropp'd) a faint sound as of running water caught my ear, and help'd me to an idea.

The sound seem'd to come from my left. Turning aside I made across the hill toward it, and after two hundred paces or so came on a tiny brook, not two feet across, that gush'd down the slope with a quite considerable chatter and impatience. The bed of it was mainly earth, with here and there a large stone or root to catch the toe: so that, as I stepped into the water and began to thread my way down between the banks of snow, 'twas necessary to look carefully to my steps.

Here and there the brook fetch'd a leap down a sharper declivity, or shot over a hanging stone: but, save for the wetting I took in these places, my progress was easy enough. I must have waded in this manner for half a mile, keeping the least possible noise, when at an angle ahead I spied a clearing among the pines, and to the right of the stream, on the very verge, a hut of logs standing, with a wood rick behind it.

'Twas a low building, but somewhat long, and I guess'd it to be, in summer time, a habitation for the woodcutters. But what surpris'd me was to hear a dull, moaning noise, very regular and disquieting, that sounded from the interior of the hut. I listen'd, and hit on the explication. 'Twas the sound of snoring.

Drawing nearer with caution, I noticed, in that end of the hut which stood over the stream, a gap, or window hole. The sound issued through this like the whirring of a dozen looms. "He must be an astonishing fellow," thought I, "that can snore in this fashion. I'll have a peep before I wake him." I waded down till I stood under the sill, put both hands upon it, and pulling myself up quiet as a mouse, stuck my face in at the window—and then very nearly sat back into the brook for fright.

For I had gazed straight down into the upturn'd faces of Captain Settle and his gang.

How long I stood there, with the water rushing past my ankles and my body turning from cold to hot, and back again, I cannot tell you. But 'twas until, hearing no pause in the sleepers' chorus, I found courage for another peep: and that must have been some time.

There were but six rascals beside the Captain (so that Jacques must have died hard, thought I), and such a raffle of arms and legs and swollen up-turn'd faces as they made I defy you to picture. For they were pack'd close as herrings; and the hut was fill'd up with their horses, ready saddled, and rubbing shoulder to loin, so narrow was the room. It needed the open window to give them air: and even so, 'twas not over-fresh inside.

I had no mind to stay: but before leaving found myself in the way of playing these villains a pretty trick. To right and left of the window, above their heads, extended two rude shelves that now were heap'd with what I conjectured to be the spoils of the larder of the "Three Cups." Holding my breath and thrusting my head and shoulders into the room, I ran my hand along and was quickly possess'd of a boil'd ham, two capons, a loaf, the half of a cold pie, and a basket holding three dozen eggs. All these prizes I filched one by one, with infinite caution.

I was gently pulling the basket through the window hole, when I heard one of the crew yawn and stretch himself in his sleep. So, determining to risk no more, I quietly pack'd the basket, slung it on my right arm, and with the ham grasp'd by the knuckle in my left, made my way up the stream.

'Twas thus laden that I enter'd the dingle, and came on the sad sight therein. I set down the ham as a thing to be asham'd of, and bar'd my head. The girl lifted her face, and turning, all white and tragical, saw me.

"My father is dead, sir."

I stoop'd and pil'd a heap of fresh snow over the blood stains. There was no intent in this but to hide the pity that chok'd me. She had still to hear about her brother, Anthony. Turning, as by a sudden thought, I took her hand. She look'd into my eyes, and her own fill'd with tears. 'Twas the human touch that loosen'd their flow, I think: and sinking down again beside her father, she wept her fill.

"Mistress Killigrew," I said, as soon as the first violence of her tears was abated, "I have still some news that is ill hearing. Your enemies are encamp'd in the woods, about a half mile below this"—and with that I told my story.

"They have done their worst, sir."

"No."

She looked at me with a question on her lip.

Said I, "you must believe me yet a short while without questioning."

Considering for a moment, she nodded. "You have a right, sir, to be trusted, tho' I know not so much as your name. Then we must stay close in hiding?" she added very sensibly, tho' with the last word her voice trail'd off, and she began again to weep.

But in time, having cover'd the dead baronet's body with sprays of the wither'd bracken, I drew her to a little distance and prevail'd on her to nibble a crust of the loaf. Now, all this while, it must be remembered, I was in my shirt sleeves, and the weather bitter cold. Which at length her sorrow allow'd her to notice.

"Why, you are shivering, sore!" she said, and running, drew my buff-coat from her father's body, and held it out to me.

"Indeed," I answer'd, "I was thinking of another expedition to warm my blood." And promising to be back in half an hour, I follow'd down my former tracks toward the stream.

Within twenty minutes I was back, running and well-nigh shouting with joy.

"Come!" I cried to her, "come and see for yourself!"

What had happen'd was this:—Wading cautiously down the brook, I had cause suddenly to prick up my ears and come to a halt. 'Twas the muffled tramp of hoofs that I heard, and creeping a bit further, I caught a glimpse, beyond the hut, of a horse and rider disappearing down the woods. He was the last of the party, as I guess'd from the sound of voices and jingling of bits further down the slope. Advancing on the hut with more boldness, I found it deserted. I scrambled up on the bank and round to the entrance. The snow before it was trampled and sullied by the footmarks of men and horses: and as I noted this, came Settle's voice calling up the slope—

"Jerry—Jerry Toy!"

A nearer voice hail'd in answer.

"Where's Reuben?"

"Coming, Captain—close behind!"

"Curse him for a loitering idiot! We've wasted time enough, as 'tis," called back the Captain. "How in thunder is a man to find the road out of this cursed wood?"

"Straight on, Cap'n—you can't miss it," shouted another voice, not two gunshots below.

A volcano of oaths pour'd up from Settle. I did not wait for the end of them: but ran back for Mistress Delia.

Together we descended to the hut. By this time the voices had faded away in distance. Yet to make sure that the rascals had really departed, we follow'd their tracks for some way, beside the stream; and suddenly came to a halt with cries of joyful surprise.

The brook had led us to a point where, over a stony fall veil'd with brown bracken, it plunged into a narrow ravine. Standing on the lip, where the water took a smoother glide before leaping, we saw the line of the ravine mark'd by a rift in the pines, and through this a slice of the country that lay below. 'Twas a level plain, well watered, and dotted here and there with houses. A range of wooded hills clos'd the view, and toward them a broad road wound gently, till the eye lost it at their base. All this was plain enough, in spite of the snow that cover'd the landscape. For the sun had burst out above, and the few flakes that still fell looked black against his brilliance and the dazzling country below.

But what caus'd our joy was to see, along the road, a small cavalcade moving away from us, with many bright glances of light and color, as their steel caps and sashes took the sunshine—a pretty sight, and the prettier because it meant our present deliverance.

The girl beside me gave a cry of delight, then sigh'd; and after a minute began to walk back toward the hut: where I left her, and ran up hill for the basket and ham. On my return, I found her examining a heap of rusty tools that, it seem'd, she had found on a shelf of the building. 'Twas no light help to the good fellowship that afterward united us, that from the first I could read her thoughts often without words; and for this reason, that her eyes were as candid as the noonday.

So now I answer'd her aloud—

"This afternoon we may venture down to the plain, where no doubt we shall find a clergyman to sell us a patch of holy ground—"

"Holy ground?" She look'd at me awhile and shook her head. "I am not of your religion," she said.

"And your father?"

"I think no man ever discovered my father's religion. Perhaps there was none to discover: but he was no bad father" she steadied her voice and went on:—"He would prefer the hillside to your 'holy ground.'"

So, an hour later, I delv'd his grave in the frosty earth, close by the spot where he lay. Somehow, I shiver'd all the while, and had a cruel shooting pain in my wound that was like to have mastered me before the task was ended. But I managed to lower the body softly into the hole and to cover it reverently from sight: and afterward stood leaning on my spade and feeling very light in the head, while the girl knelt and pray'd for her father's soul.

And the picture of her as she knelt is the last I remember, till I open'd my eyes, and was amazed to find myself on my back, and staring up at darkness.

"What has happen'd?"

"I think you are very ill," said a voice: "can you lean on me, and reach the hut?"

"Why, yes: that is, I think so. Why is everything dark?"

"The sun has been down for hours. You have been in a swoon first, and then talk'd—oh, such nonsense! Shame on me, to let you catch this chill!"

She help'd me to my feet and steadied me: and how we reached the hut I cannot tell you. It took more than one weary hour, as I now know; but, at the time, hours and minutes were one to me.

In that hut I lay four nights and four days, between ague fit and fever. And that is all the account I can give of the time, save that, on the second day, the girl left me alone in the hut and descended to the plain, where, after asking at many cottages for a physician, she was forced to be content with an old woman reputed to be amazingly well skill'd in herbs and medicines; whom, after a day's trial, she turn'd out of doors. On the fourth day, fearing for my life, she made another descent, and coming to a wayside tavern, purchased a pint of aqua vitae, carried it back, and mix'd a potion that threw me into a profuse sweat. The same evening I sat up, a sound man.

Indeed, so thoroughly was I recover'd that, waking early next morning, and finding my sweet nurse asleep from sheer weariness, in a corner of the hut, I stagger'd up from my bed of dried bracken, and out into the pure air. Rare it was to stand and drink it in like wine. A footstep arous'd me. 'Twas Mistress Delia: and turning, I held out my hand.

"Now this is famous," said she: "a day or two will see you as good a man as ever."

"A day or two? To-morrow at latest, I shall make trial to start." I noted a sudden change on her face, and added: "Indeed, you must hear my reasons before setting me down for an ingrate;" and told her of the King's letter that I carried. "I hoped that for a while our ways might lie together," said I; and broke off, for she was looking me earnestly in the face.

"Sir, as you know, my brother Anthony was to have met me—nay, for pity's sake, turn not your face away! I have guess'd—the sword you carry—I mark'd it. Sir, be merciful, and tell me!"

I led her a little aside to the foot of a tall pine; and there, tho' it rung my heart, told her all; and left her to wrestle with this final sorrow. She was so tender a thing to be stricken thus, that I who had dealt the blow crept back to the hut, covering my eyes. In an hour's time I look'd out. She was gone.

At nightfall she return'd, white with grief and fatigue; yet I was glad to see her eyes red and swol'n with weeping. Throughout our supper she kept silence; but when 'twas over, look'd up and spoke in a steady tone—

"Sir, I have a favor to ask, and must risk being held importunate—"

"From you to me," I put in, "all talk of favors had best be dropp'd."

"No—listen. If ever it befel you to lose father or mother or dearly loved friend, you will know how the anguish stuns—Oh sir! to-day the sun seem'd fallen out of heaven, and I a blind creature left groping in the void. Indeed, sir, 'tis no wonder: I had a father, brother, and servant ready to die for me—three hearts to love and lean on: and to-day they are gone."

I would have spoken, but she held up a hand.

"Now when you spoke of Anthony—a dear lad!—I lay for some time dazed with grief. By little and little, as the truth grew plainer, the pain grew also past bearing. I stood up and stagger'd into the woods to escape it. I went fast and straight, heeding nothing, for at first my senses were all confus'd: but in a while the walking clear'd my wits, and I could think: and thinking, I could weep: and having wept, could fortify my heart. Here is the upshot, sir—tho' 'tis held immodest for a maid to ask even far less of a man. We are both bound for Cornwall—you on an honorable mission, I for my father's estate of Gleys, wherefrom (as your tale proves) some unseen hands are thrusting me. Alike we carry our lives in our hands. You must go forward: I may not go back. For from a King who cannot right his own affairs there is little hope; and in Cornwall I have surer friends than he. Therefore take me, sir—take me for a comrade! Am I sad? Do you fear a weary journey? I will smile—laugh—sing—put sorrow behind me. I will contrive a thousand ways to cheat the milestones. At the first hint of tears, discard me, and go your way with no prick of conscience. Only try me—oh, the shame of speaking thus!"

Her voice had grown more rapid toward the close: and now, breaking off, she put both hands to cover her face, that was hot with blushes. I went over and took them in mine:

"You have made me the blithest man alive," said I.

She drew back a pace with a frighten'd look, and would have pull'd her hands away.

"Because," I went on quickly, "you have paid me this high compliment, to trust me. Proud was I to listen to you; and merrily will the miles pass with you for comrade. And so I say—Mistress Killigrew, take me for your servant."

To my extreme discomposure, as I dropp'd her hands, her eyes were twinkling with laughter.

"Dear now; I see a dull prospect ahead if we use these long titles!"

"But—"

"Indeed, sir, please yourself. Only as I intend to call you 'Jack' perhaps 'Delia' will be more of a piece than 'Mistress Killigrew.'" She dropp'd me a mock curtsey. "And now, Jack, be a good boy, and hitch me this quilt across the hut. I bought it yesterday at a cottage below here—"

She ended the sentence with the prettiest blush imaginable; and so, having fix'd her screen, we shook hands on our comradeship, and wish'd each other good night.

CHAPTER VIII.

I LOSE THE KING'S LETTER; AND AM CARRIED TO BRISTOL.

Almost before daylight we were afoot, and the first ray of cold sunshine found us stepping from the woods into the plain, where now the snow was vanished and a glistening coat of rime spread over all things. Down here the pines gave way to bare elms and poplars, thickly dotted, and among them the twisting smoke of farmstead and cottage, here and there, and the morning stir of kitchen and stable very musical in the crisp air.

Delia stepped along beside me, humming an air or breaking off to chatter. Meeting us, you would have said we had never a care. The road went stretching away to the northwest and the hills against the sky there; whither beyond, we neither knew nor (being both young, and one, by this time, pretty deep in love) did greatly care. Yet meeting with a waggoner and his team, we drew up to enquire.

The waggoner had a shock of whitish hair and a face purple-red above, by reason of the cold, and purple-black below, for lack of a barber. He purs'd up his mouth and look'd us slowly up and down.

"Come," said I, "you are not deaf, I hope, nor dumb."

"Send I may niver!" the fellow ejaculated, slowly and with contemplation: "'tis an unseemly sight, yet tickling to the mirthfully minded. Haw—haw!" He check'd his laughter suddenly and stood like a stone image beside his horses.

"Good sir," said Delia, laying a hand on my arm (for I was growing nettled), "your mirth is a riddle: but tell us our way and you are free to laugh."

"Oh, Scarlet—Scarlet!" answer'd he: "and to me, that am a man o' blushes from my cradle!"

Convinced by this that the fellow must be an idiot, I told him so, and left him staring after us; nor heard the sound of his horses moving on again for many minutes.

After this we met about a dozen on the road, and all paus'd to stare. But from one—an old woman—we learn'd we were walking toward Marlboro', and about noon were over the hills and looking into the valley beyond.

'Twas very like the other vale; only a pleasant stream wound along the bottom, by the banks of which the road took us. Here, by a bridge, we came to an inn bearing the sign of "The Broad Face," and entered: for Captain Settle's stock of victuals was now done. A sour-fac'd woman met us at the door.

"Do you stay here," Delia advis'd me, "and drink a mug of beer while I bargain with the hostess for fresh food." She follow'd the sour-fac'd woman into the house.

But out she comes presently with her cheeks flaming and a pair of bright eyes. "Come!" she commanded, "come at once!" Setting down my half emptied mug, I went after her across the bridge and up the road, wondering. In this way we must have walk'd for a mile or more before she turn'd and stamp'd her little foot—

"Horrible!" she cried. "Horrible—wicked—shameful! Ugh!" There were tears in her eyes.

"What is shameful?"

She made no reply, but walk'd on again quickly.

"I am getting hungry, for my part," sigh'd I, after a little.

"Then you must starve!"

"Oh!"

She wheel'd round again.

"Jack, this will never do. If you are to have a comrade, let it be a boy."

"Now, I am very passably content as things are."

"Nonsense: at Marlboro', I mean, you must buy me a suit of boy's clothes. What are you hearkening to?"

"I thought I heard the noise of guns—or is it thunder?"

"Dear Jack, don't say 'tis thunder! I do mortally fear thunder—and mice."

"'Twouldn't be thunder at this time of year. No, 'tis guns firing."

"Where?—not that I mind guns."

"Ahead of us."

On the far side of the valley we enter'd a wood, thinking by this to shorten our way: for the road here took a long bend to eastward. Now, at first this wood seem'd of no considerable size, but thicken'd and spread as we advanced. 'Twas only, however, after passing the ridge, and when daylight began to fail us, that I became alarm'd. For the wood grew denser, with a tangle of paths criss-crossing amid the undergrowth. And just then came the low mutter of cannon again, shaking the earth. We began to run forward, tripping in the gloom over brambles, and stumbling into holes.

For a mile or so this lasted: and then, without warning, I heard a sound behind me, and look'd back, to find Delia sunk upon the ground.

"Jack, here's a to-do!"

"What's amiss?"

"Why, I am going to swoon!"

The words were scarce out, when there sounded a crackling and snapping of twigs ahead, and two figures came rushing toward us—a man and a woman. The man carried an infant in his arms: and tho' I call'd on them to stop, the pair ran by us with no more notice than if we had been stones. Only the woman cried, "Dear Lord, save us!" and wrung her hands as she pass'd out of sight.

"This is strange conduct," thought I: but peering down, saw that Delia's face was white and motionless. She had swoon'd, indeed, from weariness and hunger. So I took her in my arms and stumbled forward, hoping to find the end of the wood soon. For now the rattle of artillery came louder and incessant through the trees, and mingling with it, a multitude of dull shouts and outcries. At first I was minded to run after the man and woman, but on second thought, resolv'd to see the danger before hiding from it.

The trees, in a short while, grew sparser, and between the stems I mark'd a ruddy light glowing. And then I came out on an open space upon the hillside, with a dip of earth in front; and beyond, a long ridge of pines standing up black, because of a red glare behind them; and saw that this came not from any setting sun, but was the light of a conflagration.

The glare danced and quiver'd in the sky, as I cross'd the hollow. It made even Delia's white cheek seem rosy. Up amid the pines I clamor'd, and along the ridge to where it broke off in a steep declivity. And lo! in a minute I look'd down as 'twere into the infernal pit.

There was a whole town burning below. And in the streets men were fighting, as could be told by their shouts and the rattle and blaze of musketry. For a garment of smoke lay over all and hid them: only the turmoil beat up as from a furnace, and the flames of burning thatches, and quick jets of firearms like lightning in a thundercloud. Great sparks floated past us, and over the trees at our back. A hot blast breath'd on our cheeks. Now and then you might hear a human shriek distinct amid the din, and this spoke terribly to the heart.

Now the town was Marlboro', and the attacking force a body of royal troops sent from Oxford to oust the garrison of the Parliament, which they did this same night, with great slaughter, driving the rebels out of the place, and back on the road to Bristol. Had we guess'd this, much ill luck had been spared us; but we knew nought of it, nor whether friends or foes were getting the better. So (Delia being by this time recover'd a little) we determined to pass the night in the woods, and on the morrow to give the place a wide berth.

Retreating, then, to the hollow (that lay on the lee side of the ridge, away from the north wind), I gather'd a pile of great stones, and spread my cloak thereover for Delia. To sleep was impossible, even with the will for it. For the tumult and fighting went on, and only died out about an hour before dawn: and once or twice we were troubled to hear the sound of people running on the ridge above. So we sat and talked in low voices till dawn; and grew more desperately hunger'd than ever.

With the chill of daybreak we started, meaning to get quit of the neighborhood before any espied us; and fetch'd a compass to the south without another look at Marlboro'. At the end of two hours, turning northwest again, we came to some water meadows beside a tiny river (the Kennet, as I think), and saw, some way beyond, a high road that cross'd to our side (only the bridge was now broken down), and further yet, a thick smoke curling up; but whence this came I could not see. Now we had been avoiding all roads this morning, and hiding at every sound of footsteps. But hunger was making us bold. I bade Delia crouch down by the stream's bank, where many alders grew, and set off toward this column of smoke.

By the spot where the road cross'd I noted that many men and horses had lately pass'd hereby to westward, and, by their footmarks, at a great speed. A little further, and I came on a broken musket flung against the hedge, with a nauseous mess of blood and sandy hairs about the stock of it; and just beyond was a dead horse, his legs sticking up like bent poles across the road. 'Twas here that my blood went cold on a sudden, to hear a dismal groaning not far ahead. I stood still, holding my breath, and then ran forward again.

The road took a twist that led me face to face with a small whitewashed cottage, smear'd with black stains of burning. For seemingly it had been fir'd in one or two places, only the flames had died out: and from the back, where some out-building yet smoulder'd, rose the smoke that I

90

spied. But what brought me to a stand was to see the doorway all crack'd and charr'd, and across it a soldier stretch'd—a green-coated rebel—and quite dead. His face lay among the burn'd ruins of the door, that had wofully singed his beard and hair. A stain of blood ran across the door stone and into the road.

I was gazing upon him and shuddering, when again I heard the groans. They issued from the upper chamber of the cottage. I stepped over the dead soldier and mounted the ladder that led upstairs.

The upper room was but a loft. In it were two beds, whereof one was empty. On the edge of the other sat up a boy of sixteen or thereabouts, stark naked and moaning miserably. With one hand he seem'd trying to cover a big wound that gaped in his chest: the other, as my head rose over the ladder, he stretch'd out with all the fingers spread. And this was his last effort. As I stumbled up, his fingers clos'd in a spasm of pain; his hands dropp'd, and the body tumbled back on the bed, where it lay with the legs dangling.

The poor lad must have been stabb'd as he lay asleep. For by the bedside I found his clothes neatly folded and without a speck of blood. They were clean, though coarse; so thinking they would serve for Delia, I took them, albeit with some scruples at robbing the dead, and covering the body with a sheet, made my way downstairs.

Here, on a high shelf at the foot of the ladder, I discover'd a couple of loaves and some milk, and also, lying hard by, a pair of shepherd's shears, which I took also, having a purpose for them. By this time, being sick enough of the place, I was glad to make all speed back to Delia.

She was still waiting among the leafless alders, and clapp'd her hands to see the two loaves under my arm.

Said I, flinging down the clothes, and munching at my share of the bread—

"Here is the boy's suit that you wish'd for."

"Oh, dear! 'tis not a very choice one." Her face fell.

"All the better for escaping notice."

"But—but I *like* to be notic'd!"

Nevertheless, when breakfast was done, she consented to try on the clothes. I left her eyeing them doubtfully, and stroll'd away by the river's bank. In a while her voice call'd to me—

"Oh, Jack—they do not fit at all!"

"Why, 'tis admirable!" said I, returning, and scanning her. Now this was a lie: but she took me more than ever, so pretty and comical she look'd in the dress.

"And I cannot walk a bit in them!" she pouted, strutting up and down.

"Swing your arms more, and let them hang looser."

"And my hair. Oh, Jack, I have such beautiful hair!"

"It must come off," said I, pulling the shears out of my pocket.

"And look at these huge boots!"

Indeed, this was the main trouble, for I knew they would hurt her in walking: yet she made more fuss about her hair, and only gave in when I scolded her roundly. So I took the shears and clipp'd the chestnut curls, one by one, while she cried for vexation; and took occasion of her tears to smuggle the longest lock inside my doublet.

* * * * *

But, an hour after, she was laughing again, and had learned to cock the poor country lad's cap rakishly over one eye: and by evening was walking with a swagger and longing (I know) to meet with folks. For, to spare her the sight of the ruin'd cottage, I had taken her round through the fields, and by every bypath that seem'd to lead westward. 'Twas safer to journey thus; and all the way she practic'd a man's carriage and airs, and how to wink and whistle and swing a stick. And once, when she left one of her shoes in a wet ditch, she said "d—n!" as natural as life: and then—

We jump'd over a hedge, plump into an outpost of rebels, as they sat munching their supper.

They were six in all, and must have been sitting like mice: for all I know of it is this. I had climb'd the hedge first, and was helping Delia over, when out of the ground, as it seem'd, a voice shriek'd, "Run—run!—the King's men are on us!" and then, my foot slipping, down I went on to the shoulders of a thick-set man, and well-nigh broke his neck as he turn'd to look up at me.

At first, the whole six were for running, I believe. But seeing only a lad stretch'd on his face, and a second on the hedge, they thought better of it. Before I could scramble up, one pair of hands was screw'd about my neck, another at my heels, and in a trice there we were pinion'd.

"Fetch the lantern, Zacchaeus."

'Twas quickly lit, and thrust into my face; and very foolish I must have look'd. The fellows were all clad in green coats, much soil'd with mud and powder. And they grinn'd in my face till I long'd to kick them.

"Search the malignant!" cried one. "Question him," call'd out another; and forthwith began a long interrogatory concerning the movements of his Majesty's troops, from which, indeed, I learn'd much concerning the late encounter: but of course could answer nought. 'Twas only natural they should interpret this silence for obstinacy.

"March 'em off to Captain Stubbs!"

"Halloa!" shouted a pockmarked trooper, that had his hand thrust in on my breast: "bring the lantern close here. What's this?"

'Twas, alas! the King's letter: and I bit my lip while they cluster'd round, turning the lantern's yellow glare upon the superscription.

"Lads, there's promotion in this!" shouted the thick-set man I had tumbled on (who, it seem'd, was the sergeant in the troop): "hand me the letter, there! Zacchaeus Martin and Tom Pine—you two bide here on duty: t'other three fall in about the prisoners—quick march!' The wicked have digged a pit—'"

The rogue ended up with a tag from the Psalmist.

We were march'd down the road for a mile or more, till we heard a loud bawling, as of a man in much bodily pain, and soon came to a small village, where, under a tavern lamp, by the door, was a man perch'd up on a tub, and shouting forth portions of the Scripture to some twenty or more green-coats assembled round. Our conductor pushed past these, and enter'd the tavern. At a door to the left in the passage he halted, and knocking once, thrust us inside.

The room was bare and lit very dimly by two tallow candles, set in bottles. Between these, on a deal table, lay a map outspread, and over it a man was bending, who look'd up sharply at our entrance.

He was thin, with a blue nose, and wore a green uniform like the rest: only his carriage proved him a man of authority.

This Captain Stubbs listened, you may be sure, with a bright'ning eye to the sergeant's story; and at the close fix'd an inquisitive gaze on the pair of us, turning the King's letter over and over in his hands.

"How came this in your possession?" he ask'd at length.

"That," said I, "I must decline to tell."

He hesitated a moment; then, re-seating himself, broke the seal, spread the letter upon the map, and read it slowly through. For the first time I began heartily to hope that the paper contain'd nothing of moment. But the man's face was no index of this. He read it through twice, folded it away in his breast, and turn'd to the sergeant—

"To-morrow at six in the morning we continue our march. Meanwhile keep these fellows secure. I look to you for this."

The sergeant saluted and we were led out. That night we pass'd in handcuffs, huddled with fifty soldiers in a hayloft of the inn and hearkening to their curious talk, that was half composed of Holy Writ and half of gibes at our expense. They were beaten men and, like all such, found comfort in deriding the greater misfortunes of others.

Before daylight the bugles began to sound, and we were led down to the green before the tavern door, where already were close upon five hundred gather'd, that had been billeted about the village and were now forming in order of march—a soil'd, batter'd crew, with torn ensigns and little heart in their movements. The sky began a cold drizzle as we set out, and through this saddening whether we trudged all day, Delia and I being kept well apart, she with the vanguard and I in the rear, seeing only the winding column, the dejected heads bobbing in front as they bent to the slanting rain, the cottagers that came out to stare as we pass'd; and hearing but the hoarse words of command, the low mutterings of the men, and always the monotonous *tramp-tramp* through the slush and mire of the roads.

'Tis like a bad dream to me, and I will not dwell on it. That night we pass'd at Chippenham—a small market town—and on the morrow went tramping again through worse weather, but always amid the same sights and sounds. There were moments when I thought to go mad, wrenching at my cords till my wrists bled, yet with no hope to escape. But in time, by good luck, my wits grew deaden'd to it all, and I march'd on with the rest to a kind of lugubrious singsong that my brain supplied. For hours I went thus, counting my steps, missing my reckoning, and beginning again.

Daylight was failing when the towers of Bristol grew clear out of the leaden mist in front; and by five o'clock we halted outside the walls and beside the ditch of the castle, waiting for the drawbridge to be let down. Already a great crowd had gather'd about us, of those who had come out to learn news of the defeat, which, the day before some fugitives had carried to Bristol. To their questions, as to all else, I listen'd like a man in a trance: and recall this only—that first I was shivering out in the rain and soon after was standing beside Delia, under guard of a dozen soldiers, and shaking with cold, beneath a gateway that led between the two wards of the castle. And there, for an hour at least, we kick'd our heels, until from the inner ward Captain Stubbs came striding and commanded us to follow.

Across the court we went in the rain, through a vaulted passage, and passing a screen of carved oak found ourselves suddenly in a great hall, near forty yards long (as I reckon it), and rafter'd with oak. At the far end, around a great marble table, were some ten or more gentlemen seated, who all with one accord turn'd their eyes upon us, as the captain brought us forward.

The table before them was litter'd with maps, warrants, and papers; and some of the gentlemen had pens in their hands. But the one on whom my eyes fastened was a tall, fair soldier that sat in the centre, and held his Majesty's letter, open, in his hand: who rose and bow'd to me as I came near.

"Sir," he said, "the fortune of war having given you into our hands, you will not refuse, I hope, to answer our questions."

"Sir, I have nought to tell," answer'd I, bowing in return.

With a delicate white hand he wav'd my words aside. He had a handsome, irresolute mouth, and was, I could tell, of very different degree from the merchants and lawyers beside him.

"You act under orders from the—the—"

"Anti-Christ," put in a snappish little fellow on his right.

"I do nothing of the sort," said I.

"Well, then, sir, from King Charles."

"I do not."

"Tush!" exclaim'd the snappish man, and then straightening himself up—"That boy with you—that fellow disguis'd as a countryman—look at his boots!—he's a Papist spy!"

"There, sir, you are wrong!"

"I saw him—I'll be sworn to his face—I saw him, a year back, at Douai, helping at the mass! I never forget faces."

"Why, what nonsense!" cried I, and burst out laughing.

"Don't mock at me, sir!" he thunder'd, bringing down his fist on the table. "I tell you the boy is a Papist!" He pointed furiously at Delia, who, now laughing also, answer'd him very demurely—

"Indeed, sir—"

"I saw you, I say."

"You are bold to make so certain of a Papist—"

"I saw you!"

"That cannot even tell maid from man!"

"What is meant by that?" asks the tall soldier, opening his eyes.

"Why, simply this, sir: I am no boy at all, but a girl!"

There was a minute, during which the little man went purple in the face, and the rest star'd at Delia in blank astonishment.

"Oh, Jack," she whisper'd in my ear, "I am so very, very sorrow: but I *cannot* wear these hateful clothes much longer."

She fac'd the company with a rosy blush.

"What say you to this?" ask'd Colonel Essex—for 'twas he—turning round on the little man.

"Say? What do I say? That the fellow is a Papist, too. I knew it from the first, and this proves it!"

CHAPTER IX.

I BREAK OUT OF PRISON.

You are now to be ask'd to pass over the next four weeks in as many minutes: as would I had done at the time! For I spent them in a bitter cold cell in the main tower of Bristol keep, with a chair and a pallet of straw for all my furniture, and nothing to stay my fast but the bread and water that the jailer—a sour man, if ever there were one—brought me twice a day.

This keep lies in the northwest corner of the outer ward of the castle—a mighty tall pile and strongly built, the walls (as the jailer told me) being a full twenty-five feet thick near the foundations, tho' by time you ascended to the towers this thickness had dwindled to six feet and no more. In shape 'twas a quadrilateral, a little shorter from north to south than from east to west (in which latter direction it measured sixty feet, about), and had four towers standing at the four corners, whereof mine was five fathoms higher than the rest.

Guess, then, how little I thought of escape, having but one window, a hundred feet (I do believe) above the ground, and that so narrow that, even without the iron bar across it, 'twould barely let my shoulders pass. What concern'd me more was the cold that gnaw'd me continually these winter nights, as I lay thinking of Delia (whom I had not seen since our examination), or gazing out on the patch of frosty heaven that was all my view. 'Twas thus I had heard Bristol bells ringing for Christmas in the town below.

Colonel Essex had been thrice to visit me, and always offer'd many excuses for my treatment; but when he came to question me, why of course I had nothing to tell, so that each visit but served to vex him more. Clearly I was suspected to know a great deal beyond what appear'd in the letter: and no doubt poor Anthony Killigrew had receiv'd some verbal message from His Majesty which he lived not long enough to transmit to me. As 'twas, I kept silence; and the Colonel in return would tell me nothing of what had befallen Delia.

One fine, frosty morning, then, when I had lain in this distress just four weeks, the door of my cell open'd, and there appear'd a young woman, not uncomely, bringing in my bread and water. She was the jailer's daughter, and wore a heavy bunch of keys at her girdle.

"Oh, good morning!" said I: for till now her father only had visited me, and this was a welcome change.

Instead of answering cheerfully (as I look'd for), she gave a little nod of the head, rather sorrowful, and answered:—

"Father's abed with the ague."

"Now you cannot expect me to be sorry."

"Nay," she said; and I caught her looking at me with something like compassion in her blue eyes, which mov'd me to cry out suddenly—

"I think you are woman enough to like a pair of lovers."

"Oh, aye: but where's t'other half of the pair?"

"You're right. The young gentlewoman that was brought hither with me—I know not if she loves me: but this I do know—I would give my hand to learn her whereabouts, and how she fares."

"Better eat thy loaf," put in the girl very suddenly, setting down the plate and pitcher.

'Twas odd, but I seem'd to hear a sob in her voice. However, her back was toward me as I glanc'd up. And next moment she was gone, locking the iron door behind her.

I turn'd from my breakfast with a sigh, having for the moment tasted the hope to hear something of Delia. But in a while, feeling hungry, I pick'd up the loaf beside me, and broke it in two.

To my amaze, out dropp'd something that jingled on the stone floor.

'Twas a small file: and examining the loaf again, I found a clasp-knife also, and a strip of paper, neatly folded, hidden in the bread.

"Deare Jack,

"Colonel Essex, finding no good come of his interrogatories, hath set me at large; tho' I continue under his eye, to wit, with a dowager of his acquaintance, a Mistress Finch. Wee dwell in a private house midway down St. Thomas his street, in Redcliffe: and she hath put a dismal dress upon me (Jack, 'tis *hideous*), but otherwise uses me not ill. But take care of thyself, my deare friend: for tho' the Colonel be a gentilman, he is press'd by them about him, and at our last interview I noted a mischief in his eye. Canst use this file?—(but take care: all the gates I saw guarded with troopers to-day.) This by one who hath been my friend: for whose sake tear the paper up. And beleeve your cordial, loving comrade

"D. K."

After reading this a dozen times, till I had it by heart, I tore the letter into small pieces and hid them in my pocket. This done, I felt lighter-hearted than for many a day, and (rather for employment than with any farther view) began lazily to rub away at my window bar. The file work'd well. By noon the bar was half sever'd, and I broke off to whistle a tune. 'Twas—

"Vivre en tout cas,
C'est le grand soulas—"
and I broke off to hear the key turning in my lock.

100

The jailer's daughter enter'd with my second meal. Her eyes were red with weeping.

Said I, "Does your father beat you?"

"He has, before now," she replied: "but not to-day."

"Then why do you weep?"

"Not for that."

"For what then?"

"For you—oh, dear, dear! How shall I tell it? They are going to—to—" She sat down on the chair, and sobb'd in her apron.

"What is't they are going to do?"

"To—to—h-hang you."

"The devil! When?"

"Tut-tut-to-morrow mo-horning!"

I went suddenly very cold all over. There was silence for a moment, and then I heard the noise of some one dropping a plank in the courtyard below.

"What's that?"

"The gug-gug—"

"Gallows?"

She nodded.

"You are but a weak girl," said I, meditating.

"Aye: but there's a dozen troopers on the landing below."

"Then, my dear, you must lock me up," I decided gloomily, and fell to whistling—

> "Vivre en tout cas,
> C'est le grand soulas—"

A workman's hammer in the court below chim'd in, beating out the tune, and driving the moral home. I heard a low sob behind me. The jailer's daughter was going.

"Lend me your bodkin, my dear, for a memento."

She pull'd it out and gave it to me.

"Thank you, and now good-bye! Stop: here's a kiss to take to my dear mistress. They shan't hang me, my dear."

The girl went out, sobbing, and lock'd the door after her.

I sat down for a while, feeling doleful. For I found myself extremely young to be hang'd. But soon the *whang—whang!* of the hammer below rous'd me. "Come," I thought, "I'll see what that rascal is doing, at any rate," and pulling the file from my pocket, began to attack the window bar with a will. I had no need for silence, at this great height above the ground: and besides, the hammering continued lustily.

Daylight was closing as I finish'd my task and, pulling the two pieces of the bar aside, thrust my head out at the window.

Directly under me, and about twenty feet from the ground, I saw a beam projecting, about six feet long, over a sort of doorway in the wall. Under this beam, on a ladder, was a carpenter fellow at work, fortifying it with two supporting timbers that rested on the sill of the doorway. He was merry enough over the job, and paused every now and again to fling a remark to a little group of soldiers that stood idling below, where the fellow's workbag and a great coil of rope rested by the ladder's foot.

"Reckon, Sammy," said one, pulling a long tobacco pipe from his mouth and spitting, "'tis a long while since thy last job o' the sort."

"Aye, lad: terrible disrepair this place has fall'n into. But send us a cheerful heart, say I! Instead o' the viper an' owl, shall henceforward be hangings of men an' all manner o' diversion."

I kept my head out of sight and listen'd.

"What time doth 'a swing?" ask'd another of the soldiers.

"I heard the Colonel give orders for nine o'clock to-morrow," answer'd the first soldier, spitting again.

The clock over the barbican struck four: and in a minute was being answer'd from tower after tower, down in the city.

"Four o'clock!" cried the man on the ladder: "time to stop work, and here goes for the last nail!" He drove it in and prepar'd to descend.

"Hi!" shouted a soldier, "you've forgot the rope."

"That'll wait till to-morrow. There's a staple to drive in, too. I tell you I'm dry, and want my beer."

He whipp'd his apron round his waist, and gathering up his nails, went down the ladder. At the foot he pick'd up his bag, shoulder'd the ladder, and loung'd away, leaving the coil of rope lying there. Presently the soldiers saunter'd off also, and the court was empty.

Now up to this moment I had but one idea of avoiding my fate, and that was to kill myself. 'Twas to this end I had borrow'd the bodkin of the maid. Afterward I had a notion of flinging myself from the window as they came for me. But now, as I look'd down on that coil of rope lying directly below, a prettier scheme struck me. I sat down on the floor of my cell and pull'd off my boots and stockings.

'Twas such a pretty plan that I got into a fever of impatience. Drawing off a stocking and picking out the end of the yarn, I began to unravel the knitting for dear life, until the whole lay, a heap of thread, on the floor. I then serv'd the other in the same way: and at the end had two lines, each pretty near four hundred yards in length: which now I divided into eight lines of about a hundred yards each.

With these I set to work, and by the end of twenty minutes had plaited a rope—if rope, indeed, it could be called—weak to be sure, but long enough to reach the ground with plenty to spare. Then, having bent my bodkin to the form of a hook, I tied it to the end of my cord, weighted it with a crown from my pocket, and clamber'd up to the window. I was going to angle for the hangman's rope.

'Twas near dark by this; but I could just distinguish it on the paving stones below, and looking about the court, saw that no one was astir. I wriggled first my head, then a shoulder, through the opening, and let the line run gently through my hand. There was still many yards left, that could be paid out, when I heard my coin tinkle softly on the pavement.

Then began my difficulty. A dozen times I pull'd my hook across the coil before it hitch'd; and then a full three score of times the rope slipped away before I had rais'd it a dozen yards. My elbow was raw, almost, with leaning on the sill, and I began to lose heart and head, when, to my delight, the bodkin caught and held. It had fasten'd on a kink in the rope, not far from the end. I began to pull up, hand over hand, trembling all the while like a leaf.

For I had two very reasonable fears. First, the rope might slip away and tumble before it reach'd my grasp. Secondly, it might, after all, prove a deal too short. It had look'd to me a new rope of many fathoms, not yet cut for to-morrow's purpose; but eyesight might well deceive at that distance, and surely enough I saw that the whole was dangling off the ground long before it came to my hand.

But at last I caught it, and slipping back into the room, pull'd it after me, yard upon yard. My heart went loud and fast. There was nothing to fasten it to but an iron staple in the door, that meant losing the width of my cell, some six feet. This, however, must be risk'd, and I made the end fast, lower'd the other out of window again, and climbing to a sitting posture on the window sill, thrust out my legs over the gulf.

Thankful was I that darkness had fallen before this, and hidden the giddy depths below me. I gripp'd the rope and push'd myself inch by inch through the window, and out over the ledge. For a moment I dangled, without courage to move a hand. Then, wreathing my legs round the rope, I loosed my left hand, and caught with it again some six inches lower. And so, down I went.

Minute follow'd minute, and left me still descending, six inches at a time, and looking neither above nor below, but always at the grey wall that seem'd sliding up in front of me. The first dizziness was over, but a horrible aching of the arms had taken the place of it. 'Twas growing intolerable, when suddenly my legs, that sought to close round the rope, found space only. I had come to the end.

I look'd down. A yard below my feet the beam of the gallows gleam'd palely out of the darkness. Here was my chance. I let my hands slip down the last foot or so of rope, hung for a moment, then dropp'd for the beam.

My feet miss'd it, as I intended they should; but I flung both arms out and caught it, bringing myself up with a jerk. While yet I hung clawing, I heard a footstep coming through the gateway between the two wards.

Here was a fix. With all speed and silence I drew myself up to the beam, found a hold with one knee upon it, got astride, and lay down at length, flattening my body down against the timber. Yet all the while I felt sure I must have been heard.

The footsteps drew nearer, and pass'd almost under the gallows. 'Twas an officer, for, as he pass'd, he called out—

"Sergeant Downs! Sergeant Downs!"

A voice from the guardroom in the barbican answer'd him through the darkness.

"Why is not the watch set?"

"In a minute, sir: it wants a minute to six."

"I thought the Colonel order'd it at half past five?"

In the silence that follow'd, the barbican clock began to strike, and half a dozen troopers tumbled out from the guardroom, some laughing, some grumbling at the coldness of the night. The officer return'd to the inner ward as they dispersed to their posts: and soon there was silence again, save for the *tramp-tramp* of a sentry crossing and recrossing the pavement below me.

All this while I lay flatten'd along the beam, scarce daring to breathe. But at length, when the man had pass'd below for the sixth time, I found heart to wriggle myself toward the doorway over which the gallows protruded. By slow degrees, and pausing whenever the fellow drew near, I crept close up to the wall: then, waiting the proper moment, cast my legs over, dangled for a second or two swinging myself toward the sill, flung myself off, and, touching the ledge with one toe, pitch'd forward in the room.

The effect of this was to give me a sound crack as I struck the flooring, which lay about a foot below the level of the sill. I pick'd myself up and listen'd. Outside, the regular tramp of the sentry prov'd he had not heard me; and I drew a long breath, for I knew that without a lantern he would never spy, in the darkness, the telltale rope dangling from the tower.

In the room where I stood all was right. But the flooring was uneven to the foot, and scatter'd with small pieces of masonry. 'Twas one of the many chambers in the castle that had dropp'd into disrepair. Groping my way with both hands, and barking my shins on the loose stones, I found a low vaulted passage that led me into a second chamber, empty as the first. To my delight, the door of this was ajar, with a glimmer of light slanting through the crack. I made straight toward it, and pull'd the door softly. It open'd, and show'd a lantern dimly burning, and the staircase of the keep winding past me, up into darkness.

My chance was, of course, to descend: which I did on tiptoe, hearing no sound. The stairs twisted down and down, and ended by a stout door with another lamp shining above it. After listening a moment I decided to be bold, and lifted the latch. A faint cry saluted me.

I stood face to face with the jailer's daughter.

The room was a small one, well lit, and lin'd about the walls with cups and bottles. 'Twas, as I guess'd, a taproom for the soldiers: and the girl had been scouring one of the pewter mugs when my entrance startled her. She stood up, white as if painted, and gasp'd—

"Quick—quick! Down here behind the counter for your life!"

There was scarce time to drop on my knees before a couple of troopers loung'd in, demanding mull'd beer. The girl bustled about to serve them, while the pair lean'd their elbows on the counter, and in this easy attitude began to chat.

"A shrewd night!"

"Aye, a very freezing frost! Lucky that soldiering is not all sentry work, or I for one 'ud ensue my natural trade o' plumbing. But let's be cheerful: for the voice o' the turtle is heard i' the land."

"Hey?"

The man took a pull at his hot beer before explaining.

"The turtle signifieth the Earl o' Stamford, that is to-night visiting Colonel Essex in secret: an' this is the import—war, bloody war. Mark me."

"Stirring, striving times!"

"You may say so! 'A hath fifteen thousand men, the Earl, no farther off than Taunton—why, my dear, how pale you look, to be sure!"

"'Tis my head that aches," answer'd the girl.

The men finish'd their drink, and saunter'd out. I crept from under the counter, and look'd at her.

"Father'll kill me for this!"

"Then you shall say—Is it forward or back I must go?"

"Neither." She pull'd up a trap close beside her feet, and pointed out a ladder leading down to the darkness. "The courts are full of troopers," she added.

"The cellar?"

She nodded.

"Quick! There's a door at the far end. It leads to the crypt of St. John's Chapel. You'll find the key beside it, and a lantern. Here is flint and steel." She reach'd them down from a shelf beside her. "Crouch down, or they'll spy you through the window. From the crypt a passage takes you to the governor's house. How to escape then, God knows! 'Tis the best I can think on."

I thank'd her, and began to step down the ladder. She stood for a moment to watch, leaving the trap open for better light. Between the avenue of casks and bins I stumbled toward the door and lantern that were just to be discern'd at the far end of the cellar. As I struck steel on flint, I heard the trap close: and since then have never set eyes on that kind-hearted girl.

The lantern lit, I took the key and fitted it to the lock. It turned noisily, and a cold whiff of air struck my face. Gazing round this new chamber, I saw two lines of squat pillars, supporting a low arch'd roof. 'Twas the crypt beneath the chapel, and smelt vilely. A green moisture trickled down the pillars, and dripp'd on the tombs beneath them.

At the end of this dreary place was a broken door, consisting only of a plank or two, that I easily pull'd away: and beyond, a narrow passage, over which I heard the tread of troopers plainly, as they pac'd to and fro; also the muffled note of the clock, sounding seven.

The passage went fairly straight, but was block'd here and there with fallen stones, over which I scrambled as best I could. And then, suddenly I was near pitching down a short flight of steps. I held the lantern aloft and look'd.

At the steps' foot widen'd out a low room, whereof the ceiling, like that of the crypt, rested on pillars. Between these, every inch of space was pil'd with barrels, chests, and great pyramids of round shot. In each corner lay a heap of rusty pikes. Of all this the signification was clear. I stood in the munition room of the Castle.

But what chiefly took my notice was a great door, studded with iron nails, that barr'd all exit from the place. Over the barrels I crept toward it, keeping the lantern high, in dread of firing any loose powder. 'Twas fast lock'd.

I think that, for a moment or two, I could have wept. But in a while the thought struck me that with the knife in my pocket 'twas possible to cut away the wood around the lock. "Courage!" said I: and pulling it forth, knelt down to work.

Luck in life has always used me better than my deserts. At an hour's end there I was, hacking away steadily, yet had made but little progress. And then, pressing the knife deep, I broke the blade off short. The door upon the far side was cas'd with iron.

Tramp—tramp!

'Twas the sound of man's footfall, and to the ear appear'd to be descending a flight of steps on the other side of the door. I bent my ear to the keyhole: then stepp'd to a cask of bullets that stood handy by.

I took out a dozen, felt in my pocket for Delia's kerchief that she had given me, caught up a pike from the pile stack'd in the corner, and softly blowing out my light, stood back to be conceal'd by the door, when it open'd.

The footsteps still descended. I heard an aged voice muttering—

"Shrivel my bones—ugh!—ugh! Wintry work—wintry work! Here's an hour to send a grandfatherly man a-groping for a keg o' powder!"

A wheezy cough clos'd the sentence, as a key was with difficulty fitted in the lock.

"Ugh—ugh! Sure, the lock an' I be a pair, for stiff joints."

The door creak'd back against me, and a shaft of light pierc'd the darkness.

Within the threshold, with his back to me, stood a grey-bearded servant, and totter'd so that the lantern shook in his hand. It sham'd me to lift a pike against one so weak. Instead, I dropp'd it with a clatter, and leap'd forward. The old fellow jumped like a boy, turn'd, and fac'd me with dropp'd jaw, which gave me an opportunity to thrust four or five bullets, not over roughly, into his mouth. Then, having turn'd him on his back, I strapp'd Delia's kerchief tight across his mouth, and took the lantern from his hand.

Not a word was said. Sure, the poor old man's wits were shaken, for he lay meek as a mouse, and star'd up at me, while I unstrapp'd his belt and bound his feet with it. His hands I truss'd up behind him with his own neckcloth; and catching up the lantern, left him there. I lock'd the door after me, and slip'd the key into my pocket as I sprang up the stairs beyond.

But here a light was shining, so once more I extinguish'd my lantern. The steps ended in a long passage, with a handsome lamp hanging at the uttermost end, and beneath this lamp I stepp'd into a place that fill'd me with astonishment.

'Twas, I could not doubt, the entrance hall of the governor's house. An oak door, very massive, fronted me; to left and right were two smaller doors, that plainly led into apartments of the house. Also to my left, and nigher than the door on that side, ran up a broad staircase, carpeted and brightly lit all the way, so that a very blaze fell on me as I stood. Under the first flight, close to my left shoulder, was a line of pegs with many cloaks and hats depending therefrom. Underfoot, I remember, the hall was richly tiled in squares of red and white marble.

Now clearly, this was a certain place wherein to be caught. "But," thought I, "behind one of the two doors, to left or to right, must lie the governor's room of business; and in that room—as likely as not—his keys." Which door, then, should I choose? For to stay here was madness.

While I stood pondering, the doubt was answer'd for me. From behind the right-hand door came a burst of laughter and clinking of glasses, on top of which a man's voice—the voice of Colonel Essex—call'd out for more wine.

I took a step to the door on the left, paus'd for a second or two with my hand on the latch, and then cautiously push'd it open. The chamber was empty.

'Twas a long room, with a light burning on a square centre table, and around it a mass of books, loose papers and documents strewn, seemingly without order. The floor too was litter'd with them. Clearly this was the Colonel's office.

I gave a rapid glance around. The lamp's rays scarce illumin'd the far corners; but in one of these stood a great leathern screen, and over the fireplace near it a rack was hanging, full of swords, pistols, and walking canes. Stepping toward it I caught sight of Anthony's sword, suspended there amongst the rest (they had taken it from me on the day of my examination); which now I took down and strapp'd at my side. I then chose out a pistol or two, slipped them into my sash, and advanced to the centre table.

Under the lamplight lay His Majesty's letter, open.

My hand was stretch'd out to catch it up, when I heard across the hall a door open'd, and the sound of men's voices. They were coming toward the office.

There was scarce time to slip back, and hide behind the screen, before the door latch was lifted, and two men enter'd, laughing yet.

"Business, my lord—business," said the first ('twas Colonel Essex): "I have much to do to-night."

"Sure," the other answer'd, "I thought we had settled it. You are to lend me a thousand out of your garrison—"

"Which, on my own part, I would willingly do. Only I beg you to consider, my lord, that my position here hangs on a thread. The extreme men are already against me: they talk of replacing me by Fiennes—"

"Nat Fiennes is no soldier."

"No: but he's a bigot—a stronger recommendation. Should this plan miscarry, and I lose a thousand men—"

"Heavens alive, man! It *cannot* miscarry. Hark ye: there's Ruthen of Plymouth will take the south road with all his forces. A day's march behind I shall follow—along roads to northward—parallel for a way, but afterward converging. The Cornishmen are all in Bodmin. We shall come on them with double their number, aye, almost treble. Can you doubt the issue?"

"Scarcely, with the Earl of Stamford for General."

The Earl was too far occupied to notice this compliment.

"'Twill be swift and secret," he said, "as Death himself—and as sure. Let be the fact that Hopton is all at sixes and sevens since the Marquis shipp'd for Wales: and at daggers drawn with Mohun."

Said the Colonel slowly—"Aye, the notion is good enough. Were I not in this corner, I would not think twice. Listen now: only this morning they forc'd me to order a young man's hanging, who might if kept alive be forc'd in time to give us news of value. I dar'd not refuse."

"He that you caught with the King's letter?"

"Aye—a trumpery missive, dealing with naught but summoning of the sheriff's posse and the like. There is more behind, could we but wait to get at it."

"The gallows may loosen his tongue. And how of the girl that was taken too?"

"I have her in safe keeping. This very evening I shall visit her, and make another trial to get some speech. Which puts me in mind—"

The Colonel tinkled a small hand bell that lay on the table.

The pause that followed was broken by the Earl.

"May I see the letter?"

The Colonel handed it, and tinkled the bell again, more impatiently. At length steps were heard in the hall, and a servant open'd the door.

"Where is Giles?" ask'd the Colonel. "Why are you taking his place?"

"Giles can't be found, your honor."

"Hey?"

"He's a queer oldster, your honor, an' maybe gone to bed wi' his aches and pains."

(I knew pretty well that Giles had done no such thing: but be sure I kept the knowledge safe behind my screen.)

"Then go seek him, and say—No, stop: I can't wait. Order the coach around at the barbican in twenty minutes from now—twenty minutes, mind, without fail. And say—'twill save time—the fellow's to drive me to Mistress Finch's house in St. Thomas' Street—sharp!"

As the man departed on his errand, the Earl laid down His Majesty's letter.

"Hang the fellow," he said, "if they want it: the blame, if any, will be theirs. But, in the name of Heaven, Colonel, don't fail in lending me this thousand men! 'Twill finish the war out of hand."

"I'll do it," answered the Colonel slowly.

"And I'll remember it," said the Earl. "To-morrow, at six o'clock, I set out."

The two men shook hands on their bargain and left the room, shutting the door after them.

I crept forth from behind the screen, my heart thumping on my ribs. Thus far it had been all fear and trembling with me; but now this was chang'd to a kind of panting joy. 'Twas not that I had spied the prison keys hanging near the fireplace, nor that behind the screen lay a heap of the Colonel's riding boots, whereof a pair, ready spurr'd, fitted me choicely well; but that my ears tingled with news that turn'd my escape to a matter of public welfare: and also that the way to escape lay plann'd in my head.

Shod in the Colonel's boots, I advanc'd again to the table. With sealing-wax and the Governor's seal, that lay handy, I clos'd up the King's letter, and sticking it in my breast, caught down the bunch of keys and made for the door.

The hall was void. I snatch'd down a cloak and heavy broad-brimm'd hat from one of the pegs, and donning them, slipp'd back the bolts of the heavy door. It opened without noise. Then, with a last hitch of the cloak, to bring it well about me, I stepp'd forth into the night, shutting the door quietly on my heels.

My feet were on the pavement of the inner ward. Above, one star only broke the blackness of the night. Across the court was a sentry tramping. As I walk'd boldly up, he stopped short by the gate between the wards and regarded me.

Now was my danger. I knew not the right key for the wicket: and if I fumbled, the fellow would detect me for certain. I chose one and drew nearer; the fellow look'd, saluted, stepp'd to the wicket, and open'd it himself.

"Good night, Colonel!"

I did not trust myself to answer: but passed rapidly through to the outer ward. Here, to my joy, in the arch'd passage of the barbican gate, was the carriage waiting, the porter standing beside the door; and here also, to my dismay, was a torch alight, and under it half a dozen soldiers chatting. A whisper pass'd on my approach—

"The Colonel!" and they hurried into the guardroom.

"Good evening, Colonel!" The porter bow'd low, holding the door wide.

I pass'd him rapidly, climb'd into the shadow of the coach, and drew a long breath.

Then ensued a hateful pause, as the great gates were unbarr'd. I gripp'd ray knees for impatience.

The driver spoke a word to the porter, who came round to the coach door again.

"To Mistress Finch's, is it not?"

"Ay," I muttered; "and quickly."

The coachman touched up his pair. The wheels mov'd; went quicker. We were outside the Castle.

With what relief I lean'd back as the Castle gates clos'd behind us! And with what impatience at our slow pace I sat upright again next minute! The wheels rumbled over the bridge, and immediately we were rolling easily down hill, through a street of some importance: but by this time the shutters were up along the shop fronts and very few people abroad. At the bottom we turn'd sharp to the left along a broader thoroughfare: and then suddenly drew up.

"Are we come?" I wonder'd. But no: 'twas the city gate, and here we had to wait for three minutes at least, till the sentries recogniz'd the Colonel's coach and open'd the doors to us. They stood on this side and that, presenting arms, as we rattled through; and next moment I was crossing a broad bridge, with the dark Avon on either side of me, and the vessels thick thereon, their lanterns casting long lines of yellow on the jetty water, their masts and cordage looming up against the dull glare of the city.

Soon we were between lines of building once more, shops, private dwellings and warehouses intermix'd; then pass'd a tall church; and in about two minutes more drew up again. I look'd out.

Facing me was a narrow gateway leading to a house that stood somewhat back from the street, as if slipping away from between the lines of shops that wedg'd it in on either hand. Over the grill a link was burning. I stepp'd from the coach, open'd the gate, and crossing the small court, rang at the house bell.

At first there was no answer. I rang again: and now had the satisfaction to hear a light footfall coming. A bolt was pull'd and a girl appear'd holding a candle high in her hand. Quick as thought, I stepped past her into the passage.

"Delia!"

"Jack!"

"Hist! Close the door. Where is Mistress Finch?"

"Upstairs, expecting Colonel Essex. Oh, the happy day! Come—" she led me into a narrow back room and setting down the light regarded me—"Jack, my eyes are red for thee!"

"I see they are. To-morrow I was to be hang'd."

She put her hands together, catching her breath: and very lovely I thought her, in her straight grey gown and Puritan cap.

"They have been questioning me. Didst get my letter?"

The answer was on my lip when there came a sound that made us both start.

'Twas the dull echo of a gun firing, up at the Castle.

"Delia, what lies at the back here?"

"A garden and a garden door: after these a lane leading to Redcliff Street."

"I must go, this moment."

"And I?"

She did not wait my answer, but running out into the passage, she came swiftly back with a heavy key. I open'd the window.

"Delia! De-lia!" 'Twas a woman's voice calling her, at the head of the stairs.

"Aye, Mistress Finch."

"Who was that at the door?"

I sprang into the garden and held forth a hand to Delia. "In one moment, mistress!" call'd she, and in one moment was hurrying with me across the dark garden beds. As she fitted the key to the garden gate, I heard the voice again.

"De-lia!"

'Twas drown'd in a—wild *rat-a-tat!* on the street door, and the shouts of many voices. We were close press'd.

"Now, Jack—to the right for our lives! Ah, these clumsy skirts!"

We turn'd into the lane and rac'd down it. For my part, I swore to drown myself in Avon rather than let those troopers retake me. I heard their outcries about the house behind us, as we stumbled over the frozen rubbish heaps with which the lane was bestrewn.

"What's our direction?" panted I, catching Delia's hand to help her along.

"To the left now—for the river."

We struck into a narrow side street; and with that heard a watchman bawl—

"Past nine o' the night, an' a—!"

The shock of our collision sent him to finish his say in the gutter.

"Thieves!" he yell'd.

But already we were twenty yards away, and now in a broader street, whereof one side was wholly lin'd with warehouses. And here, to our dismay, we heard shouts behind, and the noise of feet running.

About halfway down the street I spied a gateway standing ajar, and pull'd Delia aside, into a courtyard litter'd with barrels and timbers, and across it to a black empty barn of a place, where a flight of wooden steps glimmer'd, that led to an upper story. We climb'd these stairs at a run,

"Faugh! What a vile smell!"

116

The loft was pil'd high with great bales of wool, as I found by the touch, and their odor enough to satisfy an army. Nevertheless, I was groping about for a place to hide, when Delia touch'd me by the arm, and pointed.

Looking, I descried in the gloom a tall quadrilateral of purple, not five steps away, with a speck of light shining near the top of it, and three dark streaks running down the middle, whereof one was much thicker than the rest. 'Twas an open doorway; the speck, a star fram'd within it; the broad streak, a ship's mast reaching up; and the lesser ones two ends of a rope, working over a pulley above my head, and used for lowering the bales of wool on shipboard.

Advancing, I stood on the sill and look'd down. On the black water, twenty feet below, lay a three-masted trader, close against the warehouse. My toes stuck out over her deck, almost.

At first glance I could see no sign of life on board: but presently was aware of a dark figure leaning over the bulwarks, near the bows. He was quite motionless. His back was toward us, blotted against the black shadow; and the man engag'd only, it seem'd, in watching the bright splash of light flung by the ship's lantern on the water beneath him.

I resolv'd to throw myself on the mercy of this silent figure; and put out a hand to test the rope. One end of it was fix'd to a bale of wool that lay, as it had been lower'd, on the deck. Flinging myself on the other, I found it sink gently from the pulley, as the weight below moved slowly upward: and sinking with it, I held on till my feet touch'd the deck.

Still the figure in the bows was motionless.

I paid out my end of the rope softly, lowering back the bale of wool: and, as soon as it rested again on deck, signalled to Delia to let herself down.

She did so. As she alighted, and stood beside me, our hands bungled. The rope slipp'd up quickly, letting down the bale with a run.

We caught at the rope, and stopp'd it just in time: but the pulley above creak'd vociferously. I turn'd my head.

The man in the bows had not mov'd.

CHAPTER X.

CAPTAIN POTTERY AND
CAPTAIN SETTLE.

"Now either I am mad or dreaming," thought I: for that the fellow had not heard our noise was to me starkly incredible. I stepp'd along the deck toward him: not an inch did he budge. I touch'd him on the shoulder.

He fac'd round with a quick start.

"Sir," said I, quick and low, before he could get a word out—"Sir, we are in your hands. I will be plain. To-night I have broke out of Bristol Keep, and the Colonel's men are after me. Give me up to them, and they hang me to-morrow: give my comrade up, and they persecute her vilely. Now, sir, I know not which side you be, but there's our case in a nutshell."

The man bent forward, displaying a huge, rounded face, very kindly about the eyes, and set atop of the oddest body in the world: for under a trunk extraordinary broad and strong, straddled & pair of legs that a baby would have disown'd—so thin and stunted were they, and (to make it the queerer) ended in feet the most prodigious you ever saw.

As I said, this man lean'd forward, and shouted into my ear so that I fairly leap'd in the air—

"My name's Pottery—Bill Pottery, cap'n o' the *Godsend*—an' you can't make me hear, not if you bust yoursel'!"

You may think this put me in a fine quandary.

"I be deaf as nails!" bawl'd he.

'Twas horrible: for the troopers (I thought) if anywhere near, could not miss hearing him. His voice shook the very rigging.

" . . . An' o' my crew the half ashore gettin' drunk, an' the half below in a very accomplished state o' liquor: so there's no chance for 'ee to speak!"

He paus'd a moment, then roared again—

"What a pity! 'Cos you make me very curious—that you do!"

Luckily, at this moment, Delia had the sense to put a finger to her lip. The man wheel'd round without another word, led us aft over the blocks, cordage, and all manner of loose gear that encumber'd the deck, to a ladder that, toward the stern, led down into darkness. Here he sign'd to us to follow; and, descending first, threw open a door, letting out a faint stream of light in our faces. 'Twas the captain's cabin, lin'd with cupboards and lockers: and the light came from an oil lamp hanging over a narrow deal table. By this light Captain Billy scrutiniz'd us for an instant: then, from one of his lockers, brought out pen, paper, and ink, and set them on the table before me.

I caught up the pen, dipp'd it, and began to write—

"I am John Marvel, a servant of King Charles; and this night am escap'd out of Bristol Castle. If you be—"

Thus far I had written without glancing up, in fear to read the disappointment of my hopes. But now the pen was caught suddenly from my fingers, the paper torn in shreds, and there was Master Pottery shaking us both by the hand, nodding and becking, and smiling the while all over his big red face.

But he ceas'd at last: and opening another of his lockers, drew forth a horn lantern, a mallet, and a chisel. Not a word was spoken as he lit the lantern and pass'd out of the cabin, Delia and I following at his heels.

Just outside, at the foot of the steps, he stoop'd, pull'd up a trap in the flooring, and disclos'd another ladder stretching, as it seem'd, down into the bowels of the ship. This we descended carefully; and found ourselves in the hold, pinching our noses 'twixt finger and thumb.

For indeed the smell here was searching to a very painful degree: for the room was narrow, and every inch of it contested by two puissant essences, the one of raw wood, the other of bilge water. With wool the place was pil'd: but also I notic'd, not far from the ladder, several casks set on their ends; and to these the captain led us.

They were about a dozen in all, stacked close together: and Master Pottery, rolling two apart from the rest, dragg'd them to another trap and tugg'd out the bungs. A stream of fresh water gush'd from each and splash'd down the trap into the bilge below. Then, having drained them, he stay'd in their heads with a few blows of his mallet.

His plan for us was clear. And in a very few minutes Delia and I were crouching on the timbers, each with a cask inverted over us, our noses at the bungholes and our ears listening to Master Pottery's footsteps as they climb'd heavily back to deck. The rest of the casks were stack'd close round us, so that even had the gloom allow'd, we could see nothing at all.

"Jack!"

"Delia!"

"Dost feel heroical at all?"

"Not one whit. There's a trickle of water running down my back, to begin with."

"And my nose it itches; and oh, what a hateful smell! Say something to me, Jack."

"My dear," said I, "there is one thing I've been longing these weeks to say: but this seems an odd place for it."

"What is't?"

I purs'd up my lips to the bunghole, and—

"I love you," said I.

There was silence for a moment: and then, within Delia's cask, the sound of muffled laughter.

"Delia," I urg'd, "I mean it, upon my oath. Wilt marry me, sweetheart?"

"Must get out of this cask first. Oh, Jack, what a dear goose thou art!" And the laughter began again.

I was going to answer, when I heard a loud shouting overhead. 'Twas the sound of someone hailing the ship, and thought I, "the troopers are on us!"

They were, in truth. Soon I heard the noise of feet above and a string of voices speaking one after another, louder and louder. And next Master Pottery began to answer up and drown'd all speech but his own. When he ceas'd, there was silence for some minutes: after which we heard a party descend to the cabin, and the trampling of their feet on the boards above us. They remain'd there some while discussing: and then came footsteps down the second ladder, and a twinkle of light reach'd me through the bunghole of my cask.

"Quick!" said a husky voice; "overhaul the cargo here!"

I heard some half dozen troopers bustling about the hold and tugging out the bales of wool.

"Hi!" call'd Master Pottery: "an' when you've done rummaging my ship, put everything back as you found it."

"Poke about with your swords," commanded the husky voice. "What's in those barrels yonder?"

"Water, sergeant," answers a trooper, rolling out a couple.

"Nothing behind them?"

"No; they're right against the side."

"Drop 'em then. Plague on this business! 'Tis my notion they're a mile a-way, and Cap'n Stubbs no better than a fool to send us back here. He's grudging promotion, that's what he is! Hurry, there—hurry!"

Ten minutes later, the searchers were gone; and we in our casks drawing long breaths of thankfulness and strong odors. And so we crouch'd till, about midnight, Captain Billy brought us down a supper of ship's biscuit: which we crept forth to eat, being sorely cramp'd.

He could not hear our thanks: but guess'd them.

"Now say not a word! To-morrow we sail for Plymouth Sound: thence for Brittany. Hist! We be all King's men aboard the *Godsend*, tho' hearing nought I says little. Yet I have my reasoning heresies, holding the Lord's Anointed to be an anointed rogue, but nevertheless to be serv'd: just as aboard the *Godsend* I be Cap'n Billy an' you plain Jack, be your virtues what they may. An' the conclusion is—damn all mutineers an' rebels! Tho', to be sure, the words be a bit lusty for a young gentlewoman's ears."

We went back to our casks with lighter hearts. Howbeit 'twas near five in the morning, I dare say, before my narrow bedchamber allow'd me to drop asleep.

I woke to spy through my bunghole the faint light of day struggling down the hatches. Above, I heard a clanking noise, and the voices of the men hiccoughing a dismal chant. They were lifting anchor. I crawl'd forth and woke Delia, who was yet sleeping: and together we ate the breakfast that lay ready set for us on the head of a barrel.

Presently the sailors broke off their song, and we heard their feet shuffling to and fro on deck.

"Sure," cried Delia, "we are moving!"

And surely we were, as could be told by the alter'd sound of the water beneath us, and the many creakings that the *Godsend* began to keep. Once more I tasted freedom again, and the joy of living, and could have sung for the mirth that lifted my heart. "Let us but gain open sea," said I, "and I'll have tit-for-tat with these rebels!"

But alas! before we had left Avon mouth twenty minutes, 'twas another tale. For I lay on my side in that dark hold and long'd to die: and Delia sat up beside me, her hands in her lap, and her great eyes fix'd most dolefully. And when Captain Billy came down with news that we were safe and free to go on deck, we turn'd our faces from him, and said we thank'd him kindly, but had no longer any wish that way—too wretched, even, to remember his deafness.

Let me avoid, then, some miserable hours, and come to the evening, when, faint with fasting and nausea, we struggled up to the deck for air, and look'd about us.

'Twas grey—grey everywhere: the sky lead-colored, with deeper shades toward the east, where a bank of cloud blotted the coast line: the thick rain descending straight, with hardly wind enough to set the sails flapping; the sea spread like a plate of lead, save only where, to leeward, a streak of curded white crawled away from under the *Godsend's* keel.

On deck, a few sailors mov'd about, red eyed and heavy. They show'd no surprise to see us, but nodded very friendly, with a smile for our strange complexions. Here again, as ever, did adversity mock her own image.

But what more took our attention was to see a row of men stretch'd on the starboard side, like corpses, their heads in the scuppers, their legs pointed inboard, and very orderly arranged. They were a dozen and two in all, and over them bent Captain Billy with a mop in his hand, and a bucket by his side: who beckon'd that we should approach.

"Array'd in order o' merit," said he, pointing with his mop like a showman to the line of figures before him.

We drew near.

"This here is Matt. Soames, master o' this vessel—an' he's dead."

"Dead?"

"Dead-drunk, that is. O the gifted man! Come up!" He thrust the mop in the fellow's heavy face. "There now! Did he move, did he wink? 'No,' says you. O an accomplished drunkard!"

He paus'd a moment; then stirr'd up No. 2, who open'd one eye lazily, and shut it again in slumber.

"You saw? Open'd one eye, hey? That's Benjamin Halliday. The next is a black man, as you see: a man of dismal color, and hath other drawbacks natural to such. Can the Aethiop shift his skin? No, but he'll open both eyes. See there—a perfect Christian, in so far as drink can make him."

With like comments he ran down the line till he came to the last man, in front of whom he stepp'd back.

"About this last—he's a puzzler. Times I put him top o' the list, an' times at the tail. That's Ned Masters, an' was once the Reverend Edward Masters, Bachelor o' Divinity in Cambridge College; but in a tavern there fell a-talking with a certain Pelagian about Adam an' Eve, an' because the fellow turn'd stubborn, put a knife into his waistband, an' had to run away to sea: a middling drinker only, but after a quart or so to hear him tackle Predestination! So there be times after all when I sets'n apart, and says, 'Drunk, you'm no good, but half-drunk, you'm priceless.' Now there's a man—" He dropp'd his mop, and, leading us aft, pointed with admiring finger to the helmsman—a thin, wizen'd fellow, with a face like a crab apple, and a pair of piercing grey eyes half hidden by the droop of his wrinkled lids. "Gabriel Hutchins, how old be you?"

"Sixty-four, come next Martinmas," pip'd the helmsman.

"In what state o' life?"

"Drunk."

"How drunk?"

"As a lord!"

"Canst stand upright?"

"Hee-hee! Now could I iver do other?—a miserable ould worms to whom the sweet effects o' quantums be denied. When was I iver wholesomely maz'd? Or when did I lay my grey hairs on the floor, saying, 'Tis enough, an' 'tis good'? Answer me that, Cap'n Bill."

"But you hopes for the best, Gabriel."

"Aye, I hopes—I hopes."

The old man sigh'd as he brought the *Godsend* a point nearer the wind; and, as we turn'd away with the Captain, was still muttering, his sharp grey eyes fix'd on the vessel's prow.

"He's my best," said Captain Billy Pottery.

With this crew we pass'd four days; and I write this much of them because they afterward, when sober, did me a notable good turn, as you shall read toward the end of this history. But lest you should judge them hardly, let me say here that when they recovered of their stupor—as happen'd to the worst after thirty-six hours—there was no brisker, handier set of fellows on the seas. And this Captain Billy well understood: "but" (said he) "I be a collector an' a man o' conscience both, which is uncommon. Doubtless there be good sots that are not good seamen, but from such I turn my face, drink they never so prettily."

'Twas necessary I should impart some notion of my errand to Captain Billy, tho' I confin'd myself to hints, telling him only 'twas urgent I should be put ashore somewhere on the Cornish coast, for that I carried intelligence which would not keep till we reached Plymouth, a town that, besides, was held by the rebels. And he agreed readily to land me in Bude Bay: "and also thy comrade, if (as I guess) she be so minded," he added, glancing up at Delia from the paper whereon I had written my request.

She had been silent of late, beyond her wont, avoiding (I thought) to meet my eye: but answer'd simply,

"I go with Jack."

Captain Billy, whose eyes rested on her as she spoke, beckon'd me, very mysterious, outside the cabin, and winking slily, whisper'd loud enough to stun one—

"Ply her, Jack"—he had call'd me "Jack" from the first—"ply her briskly! Womankind is but yielding flesh: 'am an amorous man mysel', an' speak but that I have prov'd."

On this—for the whole ship could hear it—there certainly came the sound of a stifled laugh from the other side of the cabin door: but it did not mend my comrade's shy humor, that lasted throughout the voyage.

To be brief, 'twas not till the fourth afternoon (by reason of baffling head winds) that we stepped out of the *Godsend's* boat upon a small beach of shingle, whence, between a rift in the black cliffs, wound up the road that was to lead us inland. The *Godsend*, as we turn'd to wave our hands, lay at half a mile's distance, and made a pretty sight: for the day, that had begun with a white frost, was now turn'd sunny and still, so that looking north we saw the sea all spread with pink and lilac and hyacinth, and upon it the ship lit up, her masts and sails glowing like a gold piece. And there was Billy, leaning over the bulwarks and waving his trumpet for "Good-bye!" Thought I, for I little dream'd to see these good fellows again, "what a witless game is this life! to seek ever in fresh conjunctions what we leave behind in a hand shake." 'Twas a cheap reflection, yet it vex'd me that as we turn'd to mount the road Delia should break out singing—

"Hey! nonni—nonni—no! Is't not fine to laugh and sing When the hells of death do ring!—"

"Why, no," said I, "I don't think it": and capp'd her verse with another—

"Silly man, the cost to find Is to leave as good behind—"

"Jack, for pity's sake, stop!" She put her fingers to her ears. "What a nasty, creaking voice thou hast, to be sure!"

"That's as a man may hold," said I, nettled.

"No, indeed: yours is a very poor voice, but mine is beautiful. So listen."

She went on to sing as she went, "Green as grass is my kirtle," "Tire me in tiffany," "Come ye bearded men-at-arms," and "The Bending Rush." All these she sang, as I must confess, most delicately well, and then fac'd me, with a happy smile—

"Now, have not I a sweet voice? Why, Jack—art still glum?"

"Delia," answer'd I, "you have first to give me a reply to what, four days agone, I ask'd you. Dear girl—nay then, dear comrade—"

I broke off, for she had come to a stop, wringing her hands and looking in my face most dolefully.

"Oh, dear—oh, dear! Jack, we have had such merry times: and you are spoiling all the fun!"

We follow'd the road after this very moodily; for Delia, whom I had made sharer of the rebels' secret, agreed that no time was to be lost in reaching Bodmin, that lay a good thirty miles to the southwest. Night fell and the young moon rose, with a brisk breeze at our backs that kept us still walking without any feeling of weariness. Captain Billy had given me at parting a small compass, of new invention, that a man could carry easily in his pocket; and this from time to time I examin'd in the moonlight, guiding our way almost due south, in hopes of striking into the main road westward. I doubt not we lost a deal of time among the byways; but at length happen'd on a good road bearing south, and follow'd it till daybreak, when to our satisfaction we spied a hill in front, topp'd with a stout castle, and under it a town of importance, that we guess'd to be Launceston.

By this, my comrade and I were on the best of terms again; and now drew up to consider if we should enter the town or avoid it to the west, trusting to find a breakfast in some tavern on the way. Because we knew not with certainty the temper of the country, it seem'd best to choose this second course: so we fetch'd around by certain barren meadows, and thought ourselves lucky to hit on a road that, by the size, must be the one we sought, and a tavern with a wide yard before it and a carter's van standing at the entrance, not three gunshots from the town walls.

"Now Providence hath surely led us to breakfast," said Delia, and stepped before me into the yard, toward the door.

I was following her when, inside of a gate to the right of the house, I caught the gleam of steel, and turn'd aside to look.

To my dismay there stood near a score of chargers in this second court, saddled and dripping with sweat. My first thought was to run after Delia; but a quick surprise made me rub my eyes with wonder—

'Twas the sight of a sorrel mare among them—a mare with one high white stocking. In a thousand I could have told her for Molly.

Three seconds after I was at the tavern door, and in my ears a voice sounding that stopp'd me short and told me in one instant that without God's help all was lost.

'Twas the voice of Captain Settle speaking in the taproom; and already Delia stood, past concealment, by the open door.

" . . . And therefore, master carter, it grieves me to disappoint thee; but no man goeth this day toward Bodmin. Such be my Lord of Stamford's orders, whose servant I am, and as captain of this troop I am sent to exact them. As they displease you, his lordship is but twenty-four hours behind: you can abide him and complain. Doubtless he will hear—*ten million devils!*"

I heard his shout as he caught sight of Delia. I saw his crimson face as he darted out and gripp'd her. I saw, or half saw, the troopers crowding out after him. For a moment I hesitated. Then came my pretty comrade's voice, shrill above the hubbub—

"Jack—they have horses outside! Leave me—I am ta'en—and ride, dear lad—ride!"

In a flash my decision was taken, for better or worse. I dash'd out around the house, vaulted the gate, and catching at Molly's mane, leap'd into the saddle.

A dozen troopers were at the gate, and two had their pistols levell'd. "Surrender!"

"Be hang'd if I do!"

I set my teeth and put Molly at the low wall. As she rose like a bird in air the two pistols rang out together, and a burning pain seem'd to tear open my left shoulder. In a moment the mare alighted safe on the other side, flinging me forward on her neck. But I scrambled back, and with a shout that frighten'd my own ears, dug my heels into her flanks.

Half a minute more and I was on the hard road, galloping westward for dear life. So also were a score of rebel troopers. Twenty miles and more lay before me; and a bare hundred yards was all my start.

CHAPTER XI.

I RIDE DOWN INTO TEMPLE: AND AM WELL TREATED THERE.

And now I did indeed abandon myself to despair. Few would have given a groat for my life, with that crew at my heels; and I least of all, now that my dear comrade was lost. The wound in my shoulder was bleeding sore—I could feel the warm stream welling—yet not so sore as my heart. And I pressed my knees into the saddle flap, and wondered what the end would be.

The sorrel mare was galloping, free and strong, her delicate ears laid back, and the network of veins under her soft skin working with the heave and fall of her withers: yet—by the mud and sweat about her—I knew she must have travelled far before I mounted. I heard a shot or two fired, far up the road: tho' their bullets must have fallen short: at least, I heard none whiz past. But the rebels' shouting was clear enough, and the thud of their gallop behind.

I think that, for a mile or two, I must have ridden in a sort of swoon. 'Tis certain, not an inch of the road comes back to me: nor did I once turn my head to look back, but sat with my eyes fastened stupidly on the mare's neck. And by-and-bye, as we galloped, the smart of my wound, the heartache, hurry, pounding of hoofs—all dropp'd to an enchanting lull. I rode, and that was all.

For, swoon or no, I was lifted off earth, as it seemed, and on easy wings to an incredible height, where were no longer hedges, nor road, nor country round; but a great stillness, and only the mare and I running languidly through it.

"Ride!"

Now, at first, I thought 'twas someone speaking this in my ear, and turn'd my head. But 'twas really the last word I had heard from Delia, now after half an hour repeated in my brain. And as I grew aware of this, the dullness fell off me, and all became very distinct. And the muscles about my wound had stiffen'd—which was vilely painful: and the country, I saw, was a brown, barren moor, dotted with peat-ricks: and I cursed it.

This did me good: for it woke the fighting-man in me, and I set my teeth. Now for the first time looking back, I saw, with a great gulp of joy, I had gained on the troopers. A long dip of the road lay between me and the foremost, now topping the crest. The sun had broke through at last, and sparkled on his cap and gorget. I whistled to Molly (I could not pat her), and spoke to her softly: the sweet thing prick'd up her ears, laid them back again, and mended her pace. Her stride was beautiful to feel.

I had yet no clear idea how to escape. In front the moors rose gradually, swelling to the horizon line, and there broken into steep, jagged heights. The road under me was sound white granite and stretch'd away till lost among these fastnesses—in all of it no sign of man's habitation. Be sure I look'd along it, and to right and left, dreading to spy more troopers. But for mile on mile, all was desolate.

Now and then I caught the cry of a pewit, or saw a snipe glance up from his bed; but mainly I was busied about the mare. "Let us but gain the ridge ahead," thought I, "and there is a chance." So I rode as light as I could, husbanding her powers.

She was going her best, but the best was near spent. The sweat was oozing, her satin coat losing the gloss, the spume flying back from her nostrils—"Soh!" I called to her: "Soh! my beauty; we ride to save an army!" The loose stones flew right and left, as she reach'd out her neck, and her breath came shorter and shorter.

A mile, and another mile, we passed in this trim, and by the end of it must have spent three-quarters of an hour at the work. Glancing back, I saw the troopers scattered; far behind, but following. The heights were still a weary way ahead: but I could mark their steep sides ribb'd with boulders. Till these were passed, there was no chance to hide. The parties in this race could see each other all the way, and must ride it out.

And all the way the ground kept rising. I had no means to ease the mare, even by pulling off my heavy jack-boots, with one arm (and that my right) dangling useless. Once she flung up her head and I caught sight of her nostril, red as fire, and her poor eyes starting. I felt her strength ebbing between my knees. Here and there she blundered in her stride. And somewhere, over the ridge yonder, lay the Army of the West, and we alone could save it.

The road, for half a mile, now fetched a sudden loop, though the country on either side was level enough. Had my head been cool, I must have guessed a reason for this: but, you must remember, I had long been giddy with pain and loss of blood—so, thinking to save time, I turned Molly off the granite, and began to cut across.

The short grass and heath being still frozen, we went fairly for the first minute or so. But away behind us, I heard a shout—and it must have been loud to reach me. I learn'd the meaning when, about two hundred yards before we came on the road again, the mare's forelegs went deep, and next minute we were plunging in a black peat-quag.

Heaven can tell how we won through. It must have been still partly frozen, and perhaps we were only on the edge of it. I only know that as we scrambled up on solid ground, plastered and breathless, I looked at the wintry sun, the waste, and the tall hill tow'ring to the right of us, and thought it a strange place to die in.

For the struggle had burst open my wound again, and the blood was running down my arm and off my fingers in a stream. And now I could count every gorsebush, every stone—and now I saw nothing at all. And I heard the tinkling of bells: and then found a tune running in my head—'twas "Tire me in tiffany," and I tried to think where last I heard it.

But sweet gallant Molly must have held on: for the next thing I woke up to was a four-hol'd cross beside the road: and soon after we were over the ridge and clattering down hill.

A rough tor had risen full in front, but the road swerved to the left and took us down among the spurs of it. Now was my last lookout. I tried to sway less heavily in the saddle, and with my eyes searched the plain at our feet.

Alas! Beneath us the waste land was spread, mile upon mile: and I groaned aloud. For just below I noted a clump of roofless cabins, and beyond, upon the moors, the dotted walls of sheep-cotes, ruined also: but in all the sad-color'd leagues no living man, nor the sign of one. It was done with us. I reined up the mare—and then, in the same motion, wheeled her sharp to the right.

High above, on the hillside, a voice was calling.

I look'd up. Below the steeper ridge of the tor a patch of land had been cleared for tillage: and here a yoke of oxen was moving leisurely before a plough ('twas their tinkling bells I had heard, just now); while behind followed the wildest shape—by the voice, a woman.

She was not calling to me, but to her team: and as I put Molly at the slope, her chant rose and fell in the mournfullest singsong.

"So-hoa! Oop Comely Vean! oop, then—o-oop!"

I rose in my stirrups and shouted.

At this and the sound of hoofs, she stay'd the plough and, hand on hip, looked down the slope. The oxen, softly rattling the chains on their yoke, turn'd their necks and gazed. With sunk head Molly heaved herself up the last few yards and came to a halt with a stagger. I slipp'd out of the saddle and stood, with a hand on it, swaying.

"What's thy need, young man—that comest down to Temple wi' sword a-danglin'?"

132

The girl was a half-naked savage, dress'd only in a strip of sacking that barely reach'd her knees, and a scant bodice of the same, lac'd in front with pack thread, that left her bosom and brown arms free. Yet she appear'd no whit abash'd, but lean'd on the plough-tail and regarded me, easy and frank, as a man would.

"Sell me a horse," I blurted out: "Twenty guineas will I give for one within five minutes, and more if he be good! I ride on the King's errand."

"Then get thee back to thy master, an' say, no horse shall he have o' me—nor any man that uses horseflesh so." She pointed to Molly's knees, that were bow'd and shaking, and the bloody froth dripping from her mouth.

"Girl, for God's sake sell me a horse! They are after me, and I am hurt." I pointed up the road. "Better than I are concerned in this."

"God nor King know I, young man. But what's on thy saddle cloth, there?"

'Twas the smear where my blood had soak'd: and looking and seeing the purple mess cak'd with mud and foam on the sorrel's flank, I felt suddenly very sick. The girl made a step to me.

"Sell thee a horse? Hire thee a bedman, more like. Nay, then, lad—"

But I saw her no longer: only called "oh-oh!" twice, like a little child, and slipping my hold of the saddle, dropp'd forward on her breast.

* * * * *

Waking, I found myself in darkness—not like that of night, but of a room where the lights have gone out: and felt that I was dying. But this hardly seem'd a thing to be minded. There was a smell of peat and bracken about. Presently I heard the tramp of feet somewhere overhead, and a dull sound of voices that appear'd to be cursing.

The footsteps went to and fro, the voices muttering most of the time. After a bit I caught a word—"Witchcraft": and then a voice speaking quite close—"There's blood 'pon her hands, an' there's blood yonder by the plough." Said another voice, higher and squeaky, "there's scent behind a fox, but you don't dig it up an' take it home." The tramp passed on, and the voices died away.

By this I knew the troopers were close, and seeking me. A foolish thought came that I was buried, and they must be rummaging over my grave: but indeed I had no wish to enquire into it; no wish to move even, but just to lie and enjoy the lightness of my limbs. The blood was still running. I felt the warmth of it against my back: and thought it very pleasant. So I shut my eyes and dropp'd off again.

Then I heard the noise of shouting, far away: and a long while after that, was rous'd by the touch of a hand, thrust in against my naked breast, over my heart.

"Who is it?" I whispered.

"Joan," answered a voice, and the hand was withdrawn.

The darkness had lifted somewhat, and though something stood between me and the light, I mark'd a number of small specks, like points of gold dotted around me—

"Joan—what besides?"

"Joan's enough, I reckon: lucky for thee 'tis none else. Joan o' the Tor folks call me, but may jet be Joan i' Good Time. So hold thy peace, lad, an' cry out so little as may be."

I felt a ripping of my jacket sleeve and shirt, now clotted and stuck to the flesh. It pain'd cruelly, but I shut my teeth: and after that came the smart and delicious ache of water, as she rinsed the wound.

"Clean through the flesh, lad:—in an' out, like country dancin'. No bullet to probe nor bone to set. Heart up, soce! Thy mother shall kiss thee yet. What's thy name?"

"Marvel, Joan—Jack Marvel."

"An' marvel 'tis thou'rt Marvel yet. Good blood there's in thee, but little enow."

134

She bandaged the sore with linen torn from my shirt, and tied it round with sackcloth from her own dress. 'Twas all most gently done: and then I found her arms under me, and myself lifted as easy as a baby.

"Left arm round my neck, Jack: an' sing out if 'tis hurtin' thee."

It seemed but six steps and we were out on the bright hillside, not fifty paces from where the plough yet stood in the furrow. I caught a glimpse of a brown neck and a pair of firm red lips, of the grey tor stretching above us and, further aloft, a flock of field fare hanging in the pale sky; and then shut my eyes for the dazzle: but could still feel the beat of Joan's heart as she held me close, and the touch of her breath on my forehead.

Down the hill she carried me, picking the softest turf, and moving with an easeful swing that rather lull'd my hurt than jolted it. I was dozing, even, when a strange noise awoke me.

'Twas a high protracted note, that seem'd at first to swell up toward us, and then broke off in half a dozen or more sharp yells. Joan took no heed of them, but seeing my eyes unclose, and hearing me moan, stopped short.

"Hurts thee, lad?"

"No." 'Twas not my pain but the sight of the sinking sun that wrung the exclamation from me—"I was thinking," I muttered.

"Don't: 'tis bad for health. But bide thee still a-while, and shalt lie 'pon a soft bed."

By this time, we had come down to the road: and the yells were still going on, louder than ever. We cross'd the road, descended another slope, and came all at once on a low pile of buildings that a moment before had been hid. 'Twas but three hovels of mud, stuck together in the shape of a headless cross, the main arm pointing out toward the moor. Around the whole ran a battered wall, patched with furs; and from this dwelling the screams were issuing—

"Joan!" the voice began, "Joan—Jan Tergagle's a-clawin' my legs—Gar-rout, thou hell cat—Blast thee, let me zog! Pull'n off Joan—Jo-an!"

The voice died away into a wail; then broke out in a racket of curses. Joan stepped to the door and flung it wide. As my eyes grew used to the gloom inside, they saw this:—

A rude kitchen—the furniture but two rickety chairs, now toss'd on their faces, an oak table, with legs sunk into the earth, a keg of strong waters, tilted over and draining upon the mud floor, a ladder leading up to a loft, and in two of the corners a few bundles of bracken strewn for bedding. To the left, as one entered, was an open hearth; but the glowing peat-turves were now pitch'd to right and left over the hearthstone and about the floor, where they rested, filling the den with smoke. Under one of the chairs a black cat spat and bristled: while in the middle of the room, barefooted in the embers, crouched a man. He was half naked, old and bent, with matted grey hair and beard hanging almost to his waist. His chest and legs were bleeding from a score of scratches; and he pointed at the cat, opening and shutting his mouth like a dog, and barking out curse upon curse.

No way upset, Joan stepped across the kitchen, laid me on one of the bracken beds, and explain'd—

"That's feyther: he's drunk."

With which she turn'd, dealt the old man a cuff that stretch'd him senseless, and gathering up the turves, piled them afresh on the hearth. This done, she took the keg and gave me a drink of it. The stuff scalded me, but I thanked her. And then, when she had shifted my bed a bit, to ease the pain of lying, she righted a chair, drew it up and sat beside me. The old man lay like a log where he had fallen, and was now snoring. Presently, the fumes of the liquor, or mere faintness, mastered me, and my eyes closed. But the picture they closed upon was that of Joan, as she lean'd forward, chin on hand, with the glow of the fire on her brown skin and in the depths of her dark eyes.

136

CHAPTER XII.

HOW JOAN SAVED THE ARMY OF THE WEST; AND SAW THE FIGHT ON BRADDOCK DOWN.

But the pain of my hurt followed into my dreams. I woke with a start, and tried to sit up.

Within the kitchen all was quiet. The old savage was still stretch'd on the floor: the cat curled upon the hearth. The girl had not stirr'd: but looking toward the window hole, I saw night out side, and a frosty star sparkling far down in the west.

"Joan, what's the hour?"

"Sun's been down these four hours." She turned her face to look at me.

"I've no business lying here."

"Chose to come, lad: none axed thee, that *I* knows by."

"Where's the mare? Must set me across her back, Joan, and let me ride on."

"Mare's in stable, wi' fetlocks swelled like puddens. Chose to come, lad; an' choose or no, must bide."

"'Tis for the General Hopton, at Bodmin, I am bound, Joan; and wound or no, must win there this night."

"And that's seven mile away: wi' a bullet in thy skull, and a peat quag thy burial. For *they* went south, and thy road lieth more south than west."

"The troopers?"

"Aye, Jack: an' work I had this day wi' those same bloody warriors: but take a sup at the keg, and bite this manchet of oat cake while I tell thee."

And so, having fed me, and set my bed straight, she sat on the floor beside me (for the better hearing), and in her uncouth tongue, told how I had been saved. I cannot write her language; but the tale, in sum, was this:—

When I dropp'd forward into her arms, Joan for a moment was taken aback, thinking me dead. But (to quote her) "'no good,' said I, 'in cuddlin' a lad 'pon the hillside, for folks to see, tho' he *have* a-got curls like a wench: an' dead or 'live, no use to wait for others to make sure.'"

So she lifted and carried me to a spot hard by, that she called the "Jew's Kitchen;" and where that was, even with such bearings as I had, she defied me to discover. There was no time to tend me, whilst Molly stood near to show my whereabouts: so she let me lie, and went to lead the sorrel down to stable.

Her hand was on the bridle when she heard a *Whoop!* up the road; and there were half a dozen riders on the crest, and tearing down hill toward her. Joan had nothing left but to feign coolness, and went on leading the mare down the slope.

In a while, up comes the foremost trooper, draws rein, and pants out "Where's he to?"

"Who?" asks Joan, making out to be surprised.

"Why, the lad whose mare thou'rt leadin'?"

"Mile an' half away by now."

"How's that?"

"Freshly horsed," explains Joan.

The troopers—they were all around her by this—swore 'twas a lie; but luckily, being down in the hollow, could not see over the next ridge. They began a string of questions all together: but at last a little tun bellied sergeant call'd "Silence!" and asked the girl, "did she loan the fellow a horse?"

Here I will quote her again:—

"'Sir, to thee,' I answer'd, 'no loan at all, but fair swap for our Grey Robin.'

"'That's a lie,' he says; 'an' I won't believe thee.'

"'Might so well,' says I; 'but go to stable, an' see for thysel' (Never had grey horse to my name, Jack; but, thinks I, that's *his'n* lookout.)"

They went, did these simple troopers, to look at the stable, and sure enough, there was no Grey Robin. Nevertheless, some amongst them had logic enough to take this as something less than proof convincing, and spent three hours and more ransacking the house and barn, and searching the tor and the moors below it. I learn'd too, that Joan had come in for some rough talk—to which she put a stop, as she told me, by offering to fight any man Jack of them for the buttons on his buffcoat. And at length, about sundown, they gave up the hunt, and road away over the moors toward Warleggan, having (as the girl heard them say) to be at Braddock before night.

"Where is this Braddock?"

"Nigh to Lord Mohun's house at Boconnoc: seven mile away to the south, and seven mile or so from Bodmin, as a crow flies."

"Then go I must," cried I: and hereupon I broke out with all the trouble that was on my mind, and the instant need to save these gallant gentlemen of Cornwall, ere two armies should combine against them. I told of the King's letter in my breast, and how I found the Lord Stamford's men at Launceston; how that Ruthen, with the vanguard of the rebels, was now at Liskeard, with but a bare day's march between the two, and none but I to carry the warning. And "Oh, Joan!" I cried, "my comrade I left upon the road. Brighter courage and truer heart never man proved, and yet left by me in the rebels' hands. Alas! that I could neither save nor help, but must still ride on: and here is the issue—to lie struck down within ten mile of my goal—I, that have traveled two hundred. And if the Cornishmen be not warned to give fight before Lord Stamford come up, all's lost. Even now they be outnumber'd. So lift me, Joan, and set me astride Molly, and I'll win to Bodmin yet."

"Reckon, Jack, thou'd best hand *me* thy letter."

Now, I did not at once catch the intent of these words, so simply spoken; but stared at her like an owl.

"There's horse in stall, lad," she went on, "tho' no Grey Robin. Tearaway's the name, and strawberry the color."

"But, Joan, Joan, if you do this—feel inside my coat here, to the left—you will save an army, girl, maybe a throne! Here 'tis, Joan, see—no, not that—here! Say the seal is that of the Governor of Bristol, who stole it from me for a while: but the handwriting will be known for the King's: and no hand but yours must touch it till you stand before Sir Ralph Hopton. The King shall thank you, Joan; and God will bless you for't."

"Hope so, I'm sure. But larn me what to say, lad: for I be main thick witted."

So I told her the message over and over, till she had it by heart.

"Shan't forgit, now," she said, at length; "an' so hearken to me for a change. Bide still, nor fret thysel'. Here's pasty an' oat cake, an' a keg o' water that I'll stow beside thee. Pay no heed to feyther, an' if he wills to get drunk an' fight wi' Jan Tergagle—that's the cat—why let'n. Drunk or sober, he's no 'count."

She hid the letter in her bosom, and stepp'd to the door. On the threshold she turned—

"Jack—forgot to ax: what be all this bloodshed about?"

"For Church and King, Joan."

"H'm: same knowledge ha' I o' both—an' that's naught. But I dearly loves fair play."

She was gone. In a minute or so I heard the trampling of a horse: and then, with a scurry of hoofs, Joan was off on the King's errand, and riding into the darkness.

Little rest had I that night; but lay awake on my bracken bed and watched the burning peat-turves turn to grey, and drop, flake by flake, till only a glowing point remained. The door rattled now and then on the hinge: out on the moor the light winds kept a noise persistent as town dogs at midnight: and all the while my wound was stabbing, and the bracken pricking me till I groaned aloud.

As day began to break, the old man picked himself up, yawned and lounged out, returning after a time with fresh turves for the hearth. He noticed me no more than a stone, but when the fire was restack'd, drew up his chair to the warmth, and breakfasted on oat cake and a liberal deal of liquor. Observing him, the black cat uncoil'd, stretch'd himself, and climbing to his master's knee, sat there purring, and the best of friends. I also judged it time to breakfast: found my store:* took a bite or two, and a pull at the keg, and lay back—this time to sleep.

When I woke, 'twas high noon. The door stood open, and outside on the wall the winter sunshine was lying, very bright and clear. Indoors, the old savage had been drinking steadily; and still sat before the fire, with the cat on one knee, and his keg on the other. I sat up and strain'd my ears. Surely, if Joan had not failed, the royal generals would march out and give battle at once: and surely, if they were fighting, not ten miles away, some sound of it would reach me. But beyond the purring of the cat, I heard nothing.

I crawl'd to my feet, rested a moment to stay the giddiness, and totter'd across to the door, where I lean'd, listening and gazing south. No strip of vapor lay on the moors that stretch'd—all bathed in the most wonderful bright colors—to the lip of the horizon. The air was like a sounding board. I heard the bleat of an old wether, a mile off, upon the tors; and was turning away dejected, when, far down in the south, there ran a sound that set my heart leaping.

'Twas the crackling of musketry.

There was no mistaking it. The noise ran like wildfire along the hills: before echo could overtake it, a low rumbling followed, and then the brisker crackling again. I caught at the door post and cried, faint with the sudden joy—

"Thou angel, Joan!—thou angel!"

And then, as something took me by the throat—"Joan, Joan—to see what thou seest!"

A long time I lean'd by the door post there, drinking in the sound that now was renewed at quicker intervals. Yet, for as far as I could see, 'twas the peacefullest scene, though dreary—quiet sunshine on the hills, and the sheep dotted here and there, cropping. But down yonder, over the edge of the moors, men were fighting and murdering each other: and I yearn'd to see how the day went.

Being both weak and loth to miss a sound of it, I sank down on the threshold, and there lay, with my eyes turned southward, through a gap in the stone fence. In a while the musketry died away, and I wondered: but thought I could still at times mark a low sound as of men shouting, and this, as I learn'd after, was the true battle.

It must have been an hour or more before I saw a number of black specks coming over the ridge of hills, and swarming down into the plain toward me: and then a denser body following. 'Twas a company of horse, moving at a great pace: and I guessed that the battle was done, and these were the first fugitives of the beaten army.

On they came, in great disorder, scattering as they advanced: and now, in parts, the hill behind was black with footmen, running. 'Twas a rout, sure enough. Once or twice, on the heights, I beard a bugle blown, as if to rally the crowd: but saw nothing come of it, and presently the notes ceased, or I forgot to listen.

The foremost company of horse was heading rather to the eastward of me, to gain the high road; and the gross pass'd me by at half a mile's distance. But some came nearer, and to my extreme joy, I learn'd from their arms and shouting, what till now I had been eagerly hoping, that 'twas the rebel army thus running in rout: and tho' now without strength to kneel, I had enough left to thank God heartily.

'Twas so curious to see the plain thus suddenly fill'd with rabble, all running from the south, and the silly startled sheep rushing helter-skelter, and huddling together on the tors above, that I forgot my own likely danger if any of this revengeful crew should come upon me lying there: and was satisfied to watch them as they straggled over the moors toward the road. Some pass'd close to the cottage; but none seem'd anxious to pause there. 'Twas a glad and a sorry sight. I saw a troop of dragoons with a standard in their midst; and a drummer running behind, too far distracted even to cast his drum away, so that it dangled against his back, with a great rent where the music had been; and then two troopers running together; and one that was wounded lay down for a while within a stone's throw of me, and would not go further, till at last his comrade persuaded him; and after them a larger company, in midst of whom was a man crying, "We are sold, I tell ye, and I can point to the man!" and so passed by. There were some, too, that were galloping three stout horses in a carriage, and upon it a brass twelve pounder. But the carriage stuck fast in a quag, and so they cut the traces and left it there, where, two days after, Sir John Berkeley's dragoons found and pulled it out. And this was the fourth, I had heard, that the King's troops took in that victory.

Yet there were not above five or six hundred in all that I saw; and I guessed (as was the case) that this must be but an off-shoot, so to say, of the bigger rout that pass'd eastward through Liskeard. I was thinking of this when I heard footsteps near, and a man came panting through a gap in the wall, into the yard.

He was a big, bareheaded fellow, exceedingly flush'd with running, but unhurt, as far as I could see. Indeed, he might easily have kill'd me, and for a moment I thought sure he would. But catching sight of me, he nodded very friendly, and sitting on a heap of stones a yard or two away, began to draw off his boot, and search for a prickle, that it seem'd had got into it.

"'Tis a mess of it, yonder," said he, quietly, and jerk'd his thumb over his shoulder.

By the look of me, he could tell I was on the other side; but this did not appear to concern him.

"How has it gone?" asked I.

"Well," says he, with his nose in the boot; "we had a pretty rising ground, and the Cornishmen march'd up and whipp'd us out—that's all—and took a mort o' prisoners." He found the prickle, drew on his boot again, and asked—

"T'other side?"

I nodded.

"That's the laughing side, this day. Good evening."

And with that he went off as fast as he came.

'Twas, may be, an hour after, that another came in through the same gap: this time a lean, hawk-eyed man, with a pinch'd face and two ugly gashes—one across the brow from left eye to the roots of his hair, the other in his leg below the knee, that had sliced through boot and flesh like a scythe-cut. His face was smear'd with blood, and he carried a musket.

"Water!" he bark'd out as he came trailing into the yard. "Give me water—I'm a dead man!"

He was stepping over me to enter the kitchen, when he halted and said—

"Art a malignant, for certain!"

And before I had a chance to reply, his musket was swung up, and I felt my time was come to die.

But now the old savage, that had been sitting all day before his fire, without so much as a sign to show if he noticed aught that was passing, jump'd up with a yell and leap'd toward us. He and the cat were on the poor wretch together, tearing and clawing. I can hear their hellish outcries to this day: but at the moment they turn'd me faint. And the next thing I recall is being dragged inside by the old man, who shut the door after me and slipp'd the bolt, leaving the wounded trooper on the other side. He beat against it for some time, sobbing piteously for water: and then I heard him groaning at intervals, till he died. At least, the groans ceased; and next day he was found with his back against the cottage wall, stark and dead.

Having pulled me inside, Joan's father must have thought he had done enough: for on the floor I lay for hours, and passed from one swoon into another. He and the cat had gone back to the fire again, and long before evening both were sound asleep.

So there I lay helpless, till, at nightfall, there came the trampling of a horse outside, and then a rap on the door. The old man started up and opened it: and in rushed Joan, her eyes lit up, her breast heaving, and in her hand a naked sword.

"Church and King, Jack!" she cried, and flung the blade with a clang on to the table. "Church and King! O brave day's work, lad—O bloody work this day!"

And I swooned again.

CHAPTER XIII.

I BUY A LOOKING GLASS AT BODMIN FAIR: AND MEET WITH MR. HANNIBAL TINGCOMB.

There had, indeed, been brave work on Braddock Down that 19th of January. For Sir Ralph Hopton with the Cornish grandees had made short business of Ruthen's army—driving it headlong back on Liskeard at the first charge, chasing it through that town, and taking 1,200 prisoners (including Sir Shilston Calmady), together with many colors, all the rebel ordnance and ammunition, and most of their arms. At Liskeard, after refreshing their men, and holding next day a solemn thanksgiving to God, they divided—the Lord Mohun with Sir Ralph Hopton and Colonel Godolphin marching with the greater part of the army upon Saltash, whither Ruthen had fled and was entrenching himself; while Sir John Berkeley and Colonel Ashburnham, with a small party of horse and dragoons and the voluntary regiments of Sir Bevill Grenville, Sir Nich. Slanning, and Colonel Trevanion, turned to the northeast, toward Launceston and Tavistock, to see what account they might render of the Earl of Stamford's army; that, however, had no stomach to await them, but posted out of the county into Plymouth and Exeter.

'Twas on this expedition that two or three of the captains I have mentioned halted for an hour or more at Temple, as well to recognize Joan's extreme meritorious service, as to thank me for the part I had in bringing news of the Earl of Stamford's advance. For 'twas this, they

146

own'd, had saved them—the King's message being but an exhortation and an advertisement upon some lesser matters, the most of which were already taken out of human hands by the turn of events.

But though, as I learn'd, these gentlemen were full of compliments and professions of esteem, I neither saw nor heard them, being by this time delirious of a high fever that followed my wound. And not till three good weeks after, was I recover'd enough to leave my bed, nor, for many more, did my full strength return to me. No mother could have made a tenderer nurse than was Joan throughout this time. 'Tis to her I owe it that I am alive to write these words: and if the tears scald my eyes as I do so, you will pardon them, I promise, before the end of my tail is reach'd.

In the first days of my recovery, news came to us (I forget how) that a solemn sacrament had been taken between the parties in Devon and Cornwall, and the country was a peace. Little I cared, at the time: but was content—now spring was come—to loiter about the tors, and while watching Joan at her work, to think upon Delia. For, albeit I had little hope to see her again, my late pretty comrade held my thoughts the day long. I shared them with nobody: for tho' 'tis probable I had let some words fall in my delirium, Joan never hinted at this, and I never found out.

To Joan's company I was left: for her father, after saving my life that afternoon, took no further notice of me by word or deed; and the cat, Jan Tergagle (nam'd after a spirit that was said to haunt the moors hereabouts), was as indifferent. So with Joan I passed the days idly, tending the sheep, or waiting on her as she ploughed, or lying full length on the hillside and talking with her of war and battles. 'Twas the one topic on which she was curious (scoffing at me when I offered to teach her to read print), and for hours she would listen to stories of Alexander and Hannibal, Caesar and Joan of Arc, and other great commanders whose history I remember'd.

One evening—'twas early in May—we had climb'd to the top of the grey tor above Temple, whence we could spy the white sails of the two

Channels moving, and, stretch'd upon the short turf there, I was telling my usual tale. Joan lay beside me, her chin propp'd on one earth-stain'd hand, her great solemn eyes wide open as she listened. Till that moment I had regarded her rather as a man comrade than a girl, but now some feminine trick of gesture awoke me perhaps, for my fancy began to contrast her with Delia, and I broke off my story and sigh'd.

"Art longing to be hence?" she asked.

I felt ashamed to be thus caught, and was silent. She look'd at me and went on—

"Speak out, lad."

"Loth would I be to leave you, Joan."

"And why?"

"Why, we are good friends, I hope: and I am grateful."

"Oh, aye—wish thee'd learn to speak the truth, Jack. Art longing to be hence, and shalt—soon."

"Why, Joan, you would not have me dwell here always?"

She made no answer for a while, and then with a change of tone—

"Shalt ride wi' me to Bodmin Fair to-morrow for a treat, an' see the Great Turk and the Fat 'Ooman and hocus-pocus. So tell me more 'bout Joan the Frenchwoman."

On the morrow, about nine in the morning, we set off—Joan on the strawberry, balanced easily on an old sack, which was all her saddle; and I on Molly, that now was sound again and chafing to be so idle. As we set out, Joan's father for the first time took some notice of me, standing at the door to see us off and shouting after us to bring home some account of the wrestling. Looking back at a quarter mile's distance I saw him still fram'd in the doorway, with the cat perch'd on his shoulder.

Bodmin town is naught but a narrow street, near on a mile long, and widening toward the western end. It lies mainly along the south side of a steep vale, and this May morning as Joan and I left the moors and rode down to it from northward, already we could hear trumpets blowing, the big drum sounding, and all the bawling voices and hubbub of the

148

fair. Descending, we found the long street lin'd with booths and shows, and nigh blocked with the crowd: for the revel began early and was now in full swing. And the crew of gipsies, whifflers, mountebanks, fortune tellers, cut-purses and quacks, mix'd up with honest country faces, beat even the rabble I had seen at Wantage.

Now my own first business was with a tailor: for the clothes I wore when I rode into Temple, four months back, had been so sadly messed with blood, and afterward cut, to free them from my wound, that now all the tunic I wore was of sackcloth, contrived and stitch'd together by Joan. So I made at once for a decent shop, where luckily I found a suit to fit me, one taken (the tailor said) off a very promising young gentleman that had the misfortune to be kill'd on Braddock Down. Arrayed in this, I felt myself again, and offered to take Joan to see the Fat Woman.

We saw her, and the Aethiop, and the Rhinoceros (which put me in mind of poor Anthony Killigrew), and the Pig-fac'd Baby, and the Cudgel play; and presently halted before a Cheap Jack, that was crying his wares in a prodigious loud voice, near the town wall.

'Twas a meagre, sharp-visag'd fellow with a grey chin beard like a billy goat's; and (as fortune would have it) spying our approach, he picked out a mirror from his stock and holding it aloft, addressed us straight—

"What have we here," cries he, "but a pair o' lovers coming? and what i' my hand but a lover's hourglass? Sure the stars of heav'n must have a hand in this conjuncture—and only thirteen pence, my pretty fellow, for a glass that will tell the weather i' your sweetheart's face, and help make it fine."

There were many country fellows with their maids in the crowd, that turned their heads at this address; and as usual the women began.

"'Tis Joan o' the Tor!"

"Joan's picked up wi' a sweetheart—tee-hee!—an' us reckoned her'd forsworn mankind!"

"Who is he?"

"Some furriner, sure: that likes garlic."

"He's bought her no ribbons yet."

"How should he, poor lad; that can find no garments upon her to fasten 'em to?"

And so on, with a deal of spiteful laughter. Some of these sayings were half truth, no doubt: but the truthfullest word may be infelix. So noting a dark flush on Joan's cheek, I thought to end the scene by taking the Cheap Jack's mirror on the spot, to stop his tongue, and then drawing her away.

But in this I was a moment too late; for just as I reached up my hand with the thirteen pence, and the grinning fellow on the platform bent forward with his mirror, I heard a coarser jest, a rush in the crowd, and two heads go *crack!* together like eggs. 'Twas two of Joan's tormentors she had taken by the hair and served so: and dropping them the next instant had caught the Cheap Jack's beard, as you might a bell rope, and wrench'd him head-foremost off his stand, my thirteen pence flying far and wide. Plump he fell into the crowd, that scatter'd on all hands as Joan pummelled him: and *whack, whack!* fell the blows on the poor idiot's face, who scream'd for mercy, as though Judgment Day were come.

No one, for the minute, dared to step between them: and presently Joan looking up, with arm raised for another buffet, spied a poor Astrologer close by, in a red and yellow gown, that had been reading fortunes in a tub of black water beside him, but was now broken off, dismayed at the hubbub. To this tub she dragged the Cheap Jack and sent him into it with a round souse. The black water splashed right and left over the crowd. Then, her wrath sated, Joan faced the rest, with hands on hips, and waited for them to come on.

Not a word had she spoken, from first to last: but stood now with hot cheeks and bosom heaving. Then, finding none to take up her challenge, she strode out through the folk, and I after her, with the mirror in my hand; while the Cheap Jack picked himself out of the tub, whining, and the Astrologer wip'd his long white beard and soil'd robe.

Outside the throng was a carriage, stopp'd for a minute by this tumult, and a servant at the horses' heads. By the look of it, 'twas the coach of some person of quality; and glancing at it I saw inside an old gentleman with a grave venerable face, seated. For the moment it flash'd on me I had seen him before, somewhere: and cudgell'd my wits to think where it had been. But a second and longer gaze assured me I was mistaken, and I went on down the street after Joan.

She was walking fast and angry; nor when I caught her up and tried to soothe, would she answer me but in the shortest words. Woman's justice, as I had just learn'd, has this small defect—it goes straight enough, but mainly for the wrong object. Which now I proved in my own case.

"Where are you going, Joan?"

"To 'Fifteen Balls" stable, for my horse."

"Art not leaving the fair yet, surely!"

"That I be, tho'. Have had fairing enow—wi' a man!"

Nor for a great part of the way home would she speak to me. But meeting, by Pound Scawens (a hamlet close to the road), with some friends going to the fair, she stopp'd for a while to chat with them, whilst I rode forward: and when she overtook me, her brow was clear again.

"Am a hot headed fool, Jack, and have spoil'd thy day for thee."

"Nay, that you have not," said I, heartily glad to see her humble, for the first time in our acquaintance: "but if you have forgiven me that which I could not help, you shall take this that I bought for you, in proof."

And pulling out the mirror, I lean'd over and handed it to her.

"What i' the world be this?" she ask'd, taking and looking at it doubtfully.

"Why, a mirror."

"What's that?"

"A glass to see your face in," I explained.

"Be this my face?" She rode forward, holding up the glass in front of her. "Why, what a handsome looking gal I be, to be sure! Jack, art certain 'tis my very own face?"

"To be sure," said I amazed.

"Well!" There was silence for a full minute, save for our horses' tread on the high road. And then—

"Jack, I be powerful dirty!"

This was true enough, and it made me laugh. She looked up solemnly at my mirth (having no sense of a joke, then or ever) and bent forward to the glass again.

"By the way," said I, "did you mark a carriage just outside the crowd, by the Cheap Jack's booth?—with a white-hair'd gentleman seated inside?"

Joan nodded. "Master Hannibal Tingcomb: steward o' Gleys."

"What!"

I jumped in my saddle, and with a pull at the bridle brought Molly to a standstill.

"Of Gleys?" I cried. "Steward of Sir Deakin Killigrew that was?"

"Right, lad, except the last word. 'That *is*,' should'st rather say."

"Then you are wrong, Joan: for he's dead and buried, these five months. Where is this house of Gleys? for to-morrow I must ride there."

"'Tis easy found, then: for it stands on the south coast yonder, and no house near it: five mile from anywhere, and sixteen from Temple, due south. Shall want thee afore thou startest, Jack. Dear, now! who'd ha' thought I was so dirty?"

The cottage door stood open as we rode into the yard, and from it a faint smoke came curling, with a smell of peat. Within I found the smould'ring turves scattered about as on the day of my first arrival, and among them Joan's father stretch'd, flat on his face: only this time the eat was curl'd up quietly, and lying between the old man's shoulder blades.

"Drunk again," said Joan shortly.

But looking more narrowly, I marked a purplish stain on the ground by the old man's mouth, and turned him softly over.

"Joan," said I, "he's not drunk—he's dead!"

She stood above us and looked down, first at the corpse, then at me, without speaking for a time: at last—

"Then I reckon he may so well be buried."

"Girl," I call'd out, being shocked at this callousness, "'tis your father—and he is dead!"

"Why that's so, lad. An he were alive, shouldn't trouble thee to bury 'n."

And so, before night, we carried him up to the bleak tor side, and dug his grave there; the black cat following us to look. Five feet deep we laid him, having dug down to solid rock; and having covered him over, went silently back to the hovel. Joan had not shed a single tear.

CHAPTER XIV.

I DO NO GOOD IN THE
HOUSE OF GLEYS.

Very early next morning I awoke, and hearing no sound in the loft above (whither, since my coming, Joan had carried her bed), concluded her to be still asleep. But in this I was mistaken: for going to the well at the back to wash, I found her there, studying her face in the mirror.

"Luckily met, Jack," she said, when I was cleansed and freshly glowing: "Now fill another bucket and sarve me the same."

"Cannot you wash yourself?" I ask'd, as I did so.

"Lost the knack, I reckon. Stand thee so, an' slush the water over me."

"But your clothes!" I cried out, "they'll be soaking wet!"

"Clothes won't be worse for a wash, neither. So slush away."

Therefore, standing at three paces' distance, I sent a bucketful over her, and then another and another. Six times I filled and emptied the bucket in all: and at the end she was satisfied, and went, dripping, back to the kitchen to get me my breakfast.

"Art early abroad," she said, as we sat together over the meal.

"Yes, for I must ride to Gleys this morning."

"Shan't be sorry to miss thee for a while. Makes me feel so shy—this cleanliness." So, promising to be back by nightfall, I went presently to saddle Molly: and following Joan's directions and her warnings against quags and pitfalls, was soon riding south across the moor and well on my road to the House of Gleys.

My way leading me by Braddock Down, I turned aside for a while to examine the ground of the late fight (tho' by now little was to be seen but a piece of earthwork left unfinish'd by the rebels, and the fresh mounds where the dead were laid); and so 'twas high noon—and a dull, cheerless day—before the hills broke and let me have sight of the sea. Nor, till the noise of the surf was in my ears, did I mark the chimneys and naked grey walls of the house I was bound for.

'Twas a gloomy, savage pile of granite, perch'd at the extremity of a narrow neck of land, where every wind might sweep it, and the waves beat on three sides the cliff below. The tide was now at the full, almost, and the spray flying in my face, as we crossed the head of a small beach, forded a stream, and scrambled up the rough road to the entrance gate.

A thin line of smoke blown level from one chimney was all the sign of life in the building: for the narrow lights of the upper story were mostly shuttered, and the lower floor was hid from me by a high wall enclosing a courtlage in front. One stunted ash, with boughs tortured and bent toward the mainland, stood by the gate, which was lock'd. A smaller door, also lock'd, was let into the gate, and in this again a shuttered iron grating. Hard by, dangled a rusty bell-pull, at which I tugg'd sturdily.

On this, a crack'd bell sounded, far in the house, and scared a flock of starlings out of a disused chimney. Their cries died away presently, and left no sound but that of the gulls wailing about the cliff at my feet. This was all the answer I won.

I rang again, and a third time: and now at last came the sound of footsteps shuffling across the court within. The shutter of the grating was slipp'd back, and a voice, crack'd as the bell, asked my business.

"To see Master Hannibal Tingcomb," answered I.

"Thy name?"

"He shall hear it in time. Say that I come on business concerning the estate."

The voice mutter'd something, and the footsteps went back. I had been kicking my heels there for twenty minutes or more when they returned, and the voice repeated the question—

"Thy name?"

Being by this time angered, I did a foolish thing; which was, to clap the muzzle of my pistol against the grating, close to the fellow's nose. Singular to say, the trick serv'd me. A bolt was slipp'd hastily back and the wicket door opened stealthily.

"I want," said I, "room for my horse to pass."

Thereupon more grumbling follow'd, and a prodigious creaking of bolts and chains; after which the big gate swung stiffly back.

"Sure, you must be worth a deal," I said, "that shut yourselves in so careful."

Before me stood a strange fellow—extraordinary old and bent, with a wizen'd face, one eye only, and a chin that almost touched his nose. He wore a dirty suit of livery, that once had been canary-yellow; and shook with the palsy.

"Master Tingcomb will see the young man," he squeak'd, nodding his head; "but is a-reading just now in his Bible."

"A pretty habit," answered I, leading in Molly—"if unseasonable. But why not have said so?"

He seem'd to consider this for a while, and then said abruptly—

"Have some pasty and some good cider?"

"Why yes," I said, "with all my heart, when I have stabled the sorrel here."

He led the way across the court, well paved but chok'd with weeds, toward the stable. I found it a spacious building, and counted sixteen stalls there; but all were empty save two, where stood the horses I had seen in Bodmin the day before. Having stabled Molly, I left the place (which was thick with cobwebs) and follow'd the old servant into the house.

He took me into a great stone kitchen, and brought out the pasty and cider, but poured out half a glass only.

"Have a care, young man: 'tis a luscious, thick, seductive drink," and he chuckled.

"'Twould turn the edge of a knife," said I, tasting it and looking at him: but his one blear'd eye was inscrutable. The pasty also was mouldy, and I soon laid it down.

"Hast a proud stomach that cometh of faring sumptuously: the beef therein is our own killing," said he. "Young sir, art a man of blood, I greatly fear, by thy long sword and handiness with the firearms."

"Shall be presently," answered I, "if you lead me not to Master Tingcomb."

He scrambled up briskly and totter'd out of the kitchen into a stone corridor, I after him. Along this he hurried, muttering all the way, and halted before a door at the end. Without knocking he pushed it open, and motioning me to enter, hasten'd back as he had come.

"Come in," said a voice that seem'd familiar to me.

Though, as you know, 'twas still high day, in the room where now I found myself was every appearance of night: the shutters being closed, and six lighted candles standing on the table. Behind them sat the venerable gentleman whom I had seen in the coach, now wearing a plain suit of black, and reading in a great book that lay open on the table. I guess'd it to be the Bible; but noted that the candles had shades about them, so disposed as to throw the light, not on the page, but on the doorway where I stood.

Yet the old gentleman, having bid me enter, went on reading for a while as though wholly unaware of me: which I found somewhat nettling, so began—

"I speak, I believe, to Master Hannibal Tingcomb, steward to Sir Deakin Killigrew."

He went on, as if ending his sentence aloud: " . . . And my darling from the power of the dog." Here he paused with finger on the place and looked up. "Yes, young sir, that is my name—steward to the late Sir Deakin Killigrew."

"The late?" cried I: "Then you know—"

"Surely I know that Sir Deakin is dead: else should I be but an unworthy steward." He open'd his grave eyes as if in wonder.

"And his son, also?"

"Also his son Anthony, a headstrong boy, I fear me, a consorter with vile characters. Alas? that I should say it."

"And his daughter, Mistress Delia?"

"Alas!" and he fetched a deep sigh.

"Do you mean, sir, that she too is dead!"

"Why, to be sure-but let us talk on less painful matters."

"In one moment, sir: but first tell me—where did she die, and when? "

For my heart stood still, and I was fain to clutch the table between us to keep me from falling. I think this did not escape him, for he gave me a sharp look, and then spoke very quiet and hush'd,

"She was cruelly kill'd by highwaymen, at the 'Three Cups' inn, some miles out of Hungerford. The date given me is the 3d of December last."

With this a great rush of joy came over me, and I blurted out, delighted—

"There, sir, you are wrong! Her father was kill'd on the night of which you speak—cruelly enough, as you say: but Mistress Delia Killigrew escaped, and after the most incredible adventures—"

I was expecting him to start up with joy at my announcement; but instead of this, he gaz'd at me very sorrowfully and shook his head; which brought me to a stand.

"Sir," I said, changing my tone, "I speak but what I know: for 'twas I had the happy fortune to help her to escape, and, under God's hand, to bring her safe to Cornwall."

"Then, where is she now?"

Now this was just what I could not tell. So, standing before him, I gave him my name and a history of all my adventures in my dear comrade's company, from the hour when I saw her first in the inn at Hungerford.

Still keeping his finger on the page, he heard me to the end attentively, but with a curling of the lips toward the close, such as I did not like. And when I had done, to my amaze he spoke out sharply, and as if to a whipp'd schoolboy.

"'Tis a cock-and-bull story, sir, of which I could hope to make you ashamed. Six weeks in your company? and in boy's habit? Surely 'twas enough the pure unhappy maid should be dead—without such vile slander on her fame, and from you, that were known, sir, to have been at that inn, and on that night, with her murderers. Boy, I have evidence that, taken with your confession, would weave you a halter; and am a Justice of the Peace. Be thankful, then, that I am a merciful man; yet be abash'd."

Abash'd, indeed, I was; or at least taken aback, to see his holy indignation and the flush on his waxen cheek. Like a fool I stood staggered, and wondered dimly where I had heard that thin voice before. In the confusion of my senses I heard it say solemnly—

"The sins of her fathers have overtaken her, as the Book of Exodus proclaim'd: therefore is her inheritance wasted, and given to the satyr and the wild ass."

"And which of the twain be you, sir?"

I cannot tell what forced this violent rudeness from me, for he seem'd an honest, good man; but my heart was boiling that any should put so ill a construction on my Delia. As for him, he had risen, and was moving with dignity to the door—to show me out, as I guess. When suddenly I, that had been staring stupidly, leap'd upon him and hurled him back into his chair.

For I had marked his left foot trailing, and, by the token, knew him for the white hair'd man of the bowling-green.

"Master Hannibal Tingcomb," I spoke in his ear, "—dog and murderer! What did you in Oxford last November? And how of Captain Lucius Higgs, otherwise Captain Luke Settle, otherwise Mr. X.? Speak, before I serve you as the dog was served that night!"

I dream yet, in my sick nights, of the change that came over the vile, hypocritical knave at these words of mine. To see his pale venerable face turn green and livid, his eyeball start, his hands clutch at air—it frighten'd me.

"Brandy!" he gasped. "Brandy! there—quick—for God's sake!"

And the next moment he had slipp'd from my grasp, and was wallowing in a fit on the floor. I ran to the cupboard at which he had pointed, and finding there a bottle of strong waters, forced some drops between his teeth; and hard work it was, he gnashing at me all the time and foaming at the mouth.

Presently he ceased to writhe and bite: and lifting, I set him in his chair, where he lay, a mere limp bundle, staring and blinking. So I sat down facing him, and waited his recovery.

"Dear young sir," he began at length feebly, his fingers searching the Bible before him, from force of habit. "Kind young sir—I am an old, dying man, and my sins have found me out. Only yesterday, the physician at Bodmin told me that my days are numbered. This is the second attack, and the third will kill me."

"Well?" said I.

"If—if Mistress Delia be alive (as indeed I did not think), I will make restitution—I will confess—only tell me what to do, that I may die in peace."

Indeed, he look'd pitiable, sitting there and stammering: but I harden'd my heart to say—

"I must have a confession, then, written before I leave the room."

"But, dear young friend, you will not use it if I give up all? You will not seek my life? that already is worthless, as you see."

"Why, 'tis what you deserve. But Delia shall say when I find her—as I shall go straight to seek her. If she be lost, I shall use it—never fear: if she be found, it shall be hers to say what mercy she can discover in her heart; but I promise you I shall advise none."

The tears by this were coursing down his shrunken cheeks, but I observ'd him watch me narrowly, as though to find out how much I knew. So I pull'd out my pistol, and setting pen and paper before him, obtained at the end of an hour a very pretty confession of his sins, which lies among my papers to this day. When 'twas written and sign'd, in a weak, rambling hand, I read it through, folded it, placed it inside my coat, and prepared to take my leave.

But he called out an order to the old servant to saddle my mare, and stood softly praying and beseeching me in the courtyard till the last moment. Nor when I was mounted would anything serve but he must follow at my stirrup to the gate. But when I had briefly taken leave, and the heavy doors had creaked behind me, I heard a voice calling after me down the road—

"Dear young sir! Dear friend!—I had forgotten somewhat."

Returning, I found the gate fastened, and the iron shutter slipp'd back.

"Well?" I asked, leaning toward it.

"Dear young friend, I pity thee, for thy paper is worthless. To-day, by my advices, the army of our most Christian Parliament, more than twenty thousand strong, under the Earl of Stamford, have overtaken thy friends, the malignant gentry, near Stratton Heath, in the northeast. They are more than two to one. By this hour to-morrow, the Papists all will be running like conies to their burrows, and little chance wilt thou have to seek Delia Killigrew, much less to find her. And remember, I know enough of thy late services to hang thee: mercy then will lie in my friends' hands; but be sure I shall advise none."

And with a mocking laugh he clapp'd—to the grating in my face.

CHAPTER XV.

I LEAVE JOAN AND RIDE TO THE WARS.

You may guess how I felt at being thus properly fooled. And the worst was I could see no way to mend it; for against the barricade between us I might have beat myself for hours, yet only hurt my fists: and the wall was so smooth and high, that even by standing on Molly's back I could not—by a foot or more—reach the top to pull myself over.

There was nothing for it but to turn homewards, down the hill: which I did, chewing the cud of my folly, and finding it bitter as gall. What consoled me somewhat was the reflection that his threats were, likely enough, mere vaporing: for of any breach of the late compact between the parties I had heard nothing, and never seem'd a country more wholly given up to peace than that through which I had ridden in the morning. So recalling Master Tingcomb's late face of terror, and the confession in my pocket, I felt more cheerful. "England has grown a strange place, if I cannot get justice on this villain," thought I; and rode forward, planning a return-match and a sweet revenge.

There is no more soothing game, I believe, in the world than this of holding imaginary triumphant discourse with your enemy. Yet (oddly) it brought me but cold comfort on this occasion, my wound being too recent and galling. The sky, so long clouded, was bright'ning now, and growing serener every minute: the hills were thick with fox-gloves, the vales white with hawthorn, smelling very sweetly in the cool of the day: but I, with the bridle flung on Molly's neck, pass'd them by, thinking only of my discomfiture, and barely rousing myself to give back a "Good-day" to those that met me on the road. Nor, till we were on the downs and Joan's cottage came in sight, did I shake the brooding off.

Joan was not in the kitchen when I arrived, nor about the buildings; nor yet could I spy her anywhere moving on the hills. So, after calling to her once or twice, I stabled the mare, and set off up the tor side to seek her.

Now I must tell you that since the day of my coming I had made many attempts to find the place where Joan had then hidden me, and always fruitlessly: though I knew well whereabouts it must be. Indeed, I had thought at first I had only to walk straight to the hole: yet found after repeated trials but solid earth and boulders for my pains.

But to-day as I climb'd past the spot, something very bright flashed in my eyes and dazzled me, and rubbing them and looking, I saw a great hole in the hill—facing to the sou'-west—in the very place I had search'd for it; and out of this a beam of light glancing.

Creeping near on tiptoe, I found one huge block of granite that before had seemed bedded, among a dozen fellow-boulders, against the turf—the base resting on another well-nigh as big—was now rolled back; having been fixed to work smoothly on a pivot, yet so like nature that no eye, but by chance, could detect it. Now, who in the beginning designed this hiding place I leave you to consider; and whether it was the Jews or Phoenicians—nations, I am told, that once work'd the hills around for tin. But inside 'twas curiously paved and lined with slabs of granite, the specks of ore in which, I noted, were the points of light that had once puzzled me. And here was Joan's bower, and Joan herself inside it.

She was sitting with her back to me, in her left hand holding up the mirror, that caught the rays of the now sinking sun (and thus had dazzled me), while with her right she tried to twist into some form of knot her tresses—black, and coarse as a horse's mane—that already she had roughly braided. A pail of water stood beside her; and around lay scatter'd a score or more of long thorns, cut to the shape of hair pins.

'Tis probable that after a minute's watching I let some laughter escape me. At any rate Joan turned, spied me, and scrambled up, with an angry red on her cheek. Then I saw that her bodice was neater lac'd than usual, and a bow of yellow ribbon (fish'd up heaven knows whence) stuck in the bosom. But the strangest thing was to note the effect of this new tidiness upon her: for she took a step forward as if to cuff me by the ear (as, a day agone, she would have done), and then stopp'd, very shy and hesitating.

"Why, Joan," said I, "don't be anger'd. It suits you choicely—it does indeed."

"Art scoffing, I doubt." She stood looking heavily and askance at me.

"On my faith, no: and what a rare tiring-bower the Jew's Kitchen makes! Come, Joan, be debonair and talk to me, for I am out of luck to-day."

"Forgit it, then" (and she pointed to the sun), "whiles yet some o't is left. Tell me a tale, an thou'rt minded."

"Of what?"

"O' the bloodiest battle thou'st ever heard tell on."

So, sitting by the mouth of the Jew's Kitchen, I told her as much as I could remember out of Homer's Iliad, wondering the while what my tutor, Mr. Josias How, of Trinity College, would think to hear me so use his teaching. By-and-bye, as I warm'd to the tale, Joan forgot her new smartness; and at length, when Hector was running from Achilles round the walls, clapp'd her hands for excitement, crying, "Church an' King, lad! Oh, brave work!"

"Why, no," answered I, "'twas not for that they were fighting;" and looking at her, broke off with, "Joan, art certainly a handsome girl: give me a kiss for the mirror."

Instead of flying out, as I look'd for, she fac'd round, and answered me gravely—

"That I will not: not to any but my master."

164

"And who is that?"

"No man yet; nor shall be till one has beat me sore: him will I love, an' follow like a dog—if so be he whack me often enow'."

"A strange way to love," laughed I.

She look'd at me straight, albeit with an odd gloomy light in her eyes.

"Think so, Jack? then I give thee leave to try."

I think there is always a brutality lurking in a man to leap out unawares. Yet why do I seek excuses, that have never yet found one? To be plain, I sprang fiercely up and after Joan, who had already started, and was racing along the slope.

Twice around the tor she led me: and though I strain'd my best, not a yard could I gain upon her, for her bare feet carried her light and free. Indeed, I was losing ground, when coming to the Jew's Kitchen a second time, she tried to slip inside and shut the stone in my face.

Then should I have been prettily bemock'd, had I not, with a great effort, contrived to thrust my boot against the door just as it was closing. Wrenching it open, I laid hand on her shoulder; and in a moment she had gripp'd me, and was wrestling like a wild-cat.

Now being Cumberland-bred I knew only the wrestling of my own county, and nothing of the Cornish style. For in the north they stand well apart, and try to wear down one another's strength: whereas the Cornish is a brisker lighter play—and (as I must confess) prettier to watch. So when Joan rush'd in and closed with me, I was within an ace of being thrown, pat.

But recovering, I got her at arm's length, and held her so, while my heart ach'd to see my fingers gripping her shoulders and sinking into the flesh. I begg'd off; but she only fought and panted, and struggled to lock me by the ankles again. I could not have dream'd to find such fierce strength in a girl. Once or twice she nearly overmastered me: but at length my stubborn play wore her out. Her breath came short and fast, then fainter: and in the end, still holding her off, I turned her by the shoulders, and let her drop quietly on the turf. No thought had I any longer of kissing her; but stood back, heartily sick and ashamed of myself.

For awhile she lay, turn'd over on her side, with hands guarding her head, as if expecting me to strike her. Then gathering herself up, she came and put her hand in mine, very meekly.

"Had lik'd it better had'st thou stamped the life out o' me, a'most. But there, lad—am thine forever!"

'Twas like a buffet in the face to me. "What!" I cried.

She look'd up in my face—dear Heaven, that I should have to write it!—with eyes brimful, sick with love; tried to speak, but could only nod: and broke into a wild fit of tears.

I was standing there with her hand in mine, and a burning remorse in my heart, when I heard the clear notes of a bugle blown, away on the road to Launceston.

Looking that way, I saw a great company of horse coming down over the crest, the sun shining level on their arms and a green standard that they bore in their midst.

Joan spied them the same instant, and check'd her sobs. Without a word we flung ourselves down full length on the turf to watch.

They were more than a thousand, as I guess'd, and came winding down the road very orderly, till, being full of them, it seem'd a long serpent writhing with shiny scales. The tramp of hoofs and jingling of bits were pretty to hear.

"Rebels!" whisper'd I.

Joan nodded.

There were three regiments in all, whereof the first (and biggest) was of dragoons. So clear was the air, I could almost read the legend on their standard, and the calls of their captains were borne up to us extremely distinct.

As they rode leisurely past, I thought of Master Tingcomb's threat, and wonder'd what this array could intend. Nor, turning it over, could I find any explanation: for the Earl of Stamford's gathering, he had said, was in the northeast, and I knew such troops as the Cornish generals had to be quarter'd at Launceston. Yet here, on the near side of Launceston, was a large body of rebel horse marching quietly to the sou'-west. Where was the head or tail to it?

Turning my head as the last rider disappear'd on the way to Bodmin, I spied a squat oddly shap'd man striding down the hill very briskly: yet he look'd about him often and kept to the hollows of the ground; and was crossing below us, as it appeared, straight for Joan's cottage.

Cried I: "There is but one man in the world with such a gait—and that's Billy Pottery!"

And jumping to my feet (for he was come directly beneath us) I caught up a great stone and sent it bowling down the slope.

Bounce it went past him, missing his legs by a foot or less. The man turn'd, and catching sight of me as I stood waving, made his way up the hill. 'Twas indeed Captain Bilty: and coming up, the honest fellow almost hugg'd me for joy.

"Was seeking thee, Jack," he bawled: "learn'd from Sir Bevill where belike I might find thee. Left his lodging at Launceston this mornin', and trudged ivery foot o' the way. A thirsty land, Jack—neither horse's meat nor man's meat therein, nor a chair to sit down on: an' three women only have I kiss'd this day!" He broke off and look'd at Joan. "Beggin' the lady's pardon for sea manners and way o' speech."

"Joan," said I, "this is Billy Pottery, a good mariner and friend of mine: and as deaf as a haddock."

Billy made a leg; and as I pointed to the road where the cavalry had just disappeared, went on with a nod—

"That's so: old Sir G'arge Chudleigh's troop o' horse sent off to Bodmin to seize the High Sheriff and his *posse* there. Two hour agone I spied 'em, and ha' been ever since playin' spy."

"Then where be the King's forces?" I made shift to enquire by signs.

"March'd out o' Launceston to-day, lad—an' but a biscuit a man between 'em, poor dears—for Stratton Heath, i' the nor'-east, where the rebels be encamp'd. Heard by scouts o' these gentry bein' sent to Bodmin, and were minded to fight th' Earl o' Stamford whiles his dragooners was away. An' here's the long an' short o't: thou'rt wanted, lad, to bear a hand wi' us up yonder—an the good lady here can spare thee."

And here we both look'd at Joan—I shamefacedly enough, and Billy with a puzzled air, which he tried very delicately to hide.

She put her hand in mine.

"To fight, lad?"

I nodded my head.

"Then go," she said without a shade in her voice; and as I made no answer, went on—"Shall a woman hinder when there's fightin' toward? Only come back when thy wars be over, for I shall miss thee, Jack."

And dropping my hand she led the way down to the cottage.

Now Billy, of course, had not heard a word of this: but perhaps he gathered some import. Any way, he pull'd up short midway on the slope, scratched his head, and thunder'd—

"What a good lass!"

Joan, some paces ahead, turn'd at this and smil'd: whereat, having no idea he'd spoken above a whisper, Billy blush'd red as any peony.

'Twas but a short half hour when, the mare being saddled and Billy fed, we took our leave of Joan. Billy walked beside one stirrup, and the girl on the other side, to see us a few yards on our way. At length she halted—

"No leave-takin's, Jack, but 'Church and King!' Only do thy best and not disgrace me."

And "Church and King!" she call'd thrice after us, standing in the road. For me, as I rode up out of that valley, the drums seem'd beating and the bugles calling to a new life ahead. The last light of day was on the tors, the air blowing fresher as we mounted: and with Molly's every step the past five months appear'd to dissolve and fall away from me as a dream.

On the crest, I turn'd in the saddle. Joan was yet standing there, a black speck on the road. She waved her hand once.

Billy had turn'd too, and, uncovering, shouted so that the hilltops echoed.

"A good lass—a good lass! But what's become o' t'other one?"

CHAPTER XVI.

THE BATTLE OF STAMFORD HEATH.

Night came, and found us but midway between Temple and Lannceston: for tho' my comrade stepp'd briskly beside me, 'twas useless to put Molly beyond a walk; and besides, the mare was new from her day's journey. This troubled me the less by reason of the moon (now almost at the full), and the extreme whiteness of the road underfoot, so that there was no fear of going astray. And Billy engaged that by sunrise we should be in sight of the King's troops.

"Nay, Jack," he said, when by signs I offered him to ride and tie: "never rode o' horseback but once, and then 'pon Parson Spinks his red mare at Bideford. Parson i' those days was courtin' the Widow Hambly, over to Torrington: an' I, that wanted to fare to Barnstaple, spent that mornin' an' better part o' th' afternoon, clawin' off Torrington. And th' end was the larboard halyards broke, an' the mare gybed, an' to Torrington I went before the wind, wi' an unseemly bloody nose. 'Lud!' cries the widow, "tis the wrong man 'pon the right horse!' 'Pardon, mistress,' says I, 'the man is well enow, but 'pon the wrong horse, for sure.'"

Now and then, as we went, I would dismount and lead Molly by the bridle for a mile or so: and all the way to Launceston Billy was recounting his adventures since our parting. It appeared that, after leaving me, they had come to Plymouth with a fair passage: but before they could unlade, had advertisement of the Governor's design to seize all vessels then riding in the Sound, for purposes of war; and so made a quick escape by night into Looe Haven, where they had the fortune to part with the best part of their cargo at a high profit. 'Twas while unlading here that Billy had a mind to pay a debt he ow'd to a cousin of his at Altarnun, and, leaving Matt Soames in charge, had tramped northward through Liskeard to Launceston, where he found the Cornish forces, and was met by the news of the Earl of Stamford's advance in the northeast. Further, meeting, in Sir Bevill's troop, with some north coast men of his acquaintance, he fell to talking, and so learn'd about me and my ride toward Braddock, which (it seem'd) was now become common knowledge. This led him to seek Sir Bevill, with the result that you know: "for," as he wound up, "'tis a desirable an' rare delight to pay a debt an' see some fun, together."

We had some trouble at Launceston gate, where were a few burghers posted for sentries, and, as I could see, ready to take fright at their own shadows. But Billy gave the watchword ("One and All"), and presently they let us through. As we pass'd along the street we marked a light in every window almost, tho' 'twas near midnight; and the people moving about behind their curtains. There were groups too in the dark doorways, gather'd there discussing, that eyed us as we went by, and answered Billy's *Good-night, honest men!* very hoarse and doubtfully.

But when we were beyond the town, and between hedges again, I think I must have dozed off in my saddle. For, though this was a road full of sharp memories, being the last I had traveled with Delia, I have no remembrance to have felt them; or, indeed, of noting aught but the fresh night air, and the constellation of the Bear blazing ahead, and Billy's voice resonant beside me.

And after this I can recall passing the tower of Marham Church, with the paling sky behind it, and some birds chattering in the carved courses: and soon (it seem'd) felt Billy's grip on my knee, and open'd my eyes to see his finger pointing.

We stood on a ridge above a hollow vale into which the sun, though now bright, did not yet pierce, but passing over to a high, conical hill beyond, smote level on line after line of white tents—the prettiest sight!

'Twas the enemy there encamped on the top and some way down the sides, the smoke of their trampled watch fires still curling among the gorsebushes. I heard their trumpets calling and drums beating to arms; for though, glancing back at the sun, I judged it to be hardly past four in the morning, yet already the slopes were moving like an ant-hill—the regiments gathering, arms flashing, horsemen galloping to and fro, and the captains shouting their commands. In the distance this had a sweet and cheerful sound, no more disquieting than a ploughboy calling to his team.

Looking down into the valley at our feet, at first I saw no sign of our own troops—only the roofs of a little town, with overmuch smoke spread above it, like a morning mist. But here also I heard the church bells clashing and a drum beating, and presently spied a gleam of arms down among the trees, and then a regiment of foot moving westward along the base of the hill. 'Twas evident the battle was at hand, and we quicken'd our pace down into the street.

It lay on the slope, and midway down we pass'd some watch fires burn'd out; and then a soldier or two running and fastening their straps; and last a little child, that seem'd wild with the joy of living amid great events, but led us pretty straight to the sign of "The Tree," which indeed was the only tavern.

It stood some way back from the street, with a great elm before the porch: where by a table sat two men, with tankards beside them, and a small company of grooms and soldiers standing round. Both men were more than ordinary tall and soldier like: only the bigger wore a scarlet cloak very richly lac'd, and was shouting orders to his men; while the other, dress'd in plain buff suit and jack boots, had a map spread before him, which he studied very attentively, writing therein with a quill pen.

"What a plague have we here?" cries the big man, as we drew up.

"Recruits if it please you, sir," said I, dismounting and pulling off my hat, tho' his insolent tone offended me.

"S'lid! The boy speaks as if he were a regiment," growls he, half aloud: "Can'st fight?"

"That, with your leave, sir, is what I am come to try."

"And this rascal?" He turned on Billy.

Billy heard not a word, of course, yet answered readily—

"Why, since your honor is so pleasantly minded—let it be cider."

Now the first effect of this, deliver'd with all force of lung, was to make the big man sit bolt upright and staring: recovering speech, however, he broke into a volley of blasphemous curses.

All this while the man in buff had scarce lifted his eyes off the map. But now he looks up—and I saw at the first glance that the two men hated each other.

"I think," said he quietly, "my Lord Mohun has forgot to ask the *gentleman's* name."

"My name is Marvel, sir—John Marvel." I answer'd him with a bow.

"Hey!"—and dropping his pen he starts up and grasps my hand—"Then 'tis you I have never thanked for His Gracious Majesty's letter."

"The General Hopton?" cried I.

"Even so, sir. My lord," he went on, still holding my hand and turning to his companion, "let me present to you the gentleman that in January sav'd your house of Bocconnoc from burning at the hands of the rebels—whom God confound this day!" He lifted his hat.

"Amen," said I, as his lordship bowed, exceedingly sulky. But I did not value his rage, being hot with joy to be so beprais'd by the first captain (as I yet hold) on the royal side. Who now, not without a sly triumph, flung the price of Billy's cider on the table and, folding up his map, address'd me again—

"Master Marvel, the fight to-day will lie but little with the horse—or so I hope. You will do well, if your wish be to serve us best, to leave your mare behind. The troop which my Lord Mohun and I command together is below. But Sir Bevill Grenville, who has seen and is interested in you, has the first claim: and I would not deny you the delight to fight your first battle under so good a master. His men are, with Sir John Berkeley's troop, a little to the westward: and if you are ready I will go some distance with you, and put you in the way to find him. My lord, may we look for you presently?"

The Lord Mohun nodded, surly enough: so, Billy's cider being now drunk and Molly given over to an ostler, we set out down the hill together, Billy shouldering a pipe and walking after with the groom that led Sir Ralph's horse. Be sure the General's courtly manner of speech set my blood tingling. I seem'd to grow a full two inches taller; and when, in the vale, we parted, he directing me to the left, where through a gap I could see Sir Bevill's troop forming at some five hundred paces' distance, I felt a very desperate warrior indeed; and set off at a run, with Billy behind me.

'Twas an open space we had to cross, dotted with gorsebushes; and the enemy's regiments, plain to see, drawn up in battalia on the slope above, which here was gentler than to the south and west. But hardly had we gone ten yards than I saw a puff of white smoke above, then another, and then the summit ring'd with flame; and heard the noise of it roaring in the hills around. At the first sound I pull'd up, and then began running again at full speed: for I saw our division already in motion, and advancing up the hill at a quick pace.

The curve of the slope hid all but the nearest: but above them I saw a steep earthwork, and thereon three or four brass pieces of ordnance glittering whenever the smoke lifted. For here the artillery was plying the briskest, pouring down volley on volley; and four regiments at least stood mass'd behind, ready to fall on the Cornish-men; who, answering with a small discharge of musketry, now ran forward more nimbly.

To catch up with them, I must now turn my course obliquely up the hill, where running was pretty toilsome. We were panting along when suddenly a shower of sand and earth was dash'd in my face, spattering me all over. Half-blinded, I look'd and saw a great round shot had ploughed a trench in the ground at my feet, and lay there buried.

At the same moment, Billy, who was running at my shoulder, plumps down on his knees and begins to whine and moan most pitiably.

"Art hurt, dear fellow?" asked I, turning.

"Oh, Jack, Jack—I have no stomach for this! A cool, wet death at sea I do not fear; only to have the great hot shot burning in a man's belly— 'tis terrifying. I *hate* a swift death! Jack, I be a sinner—I will confess: I lied to thee yesterday—never kiss'd the three maids I spoke of—never kiss'd but one i' my life, an' her a tap-wench, that slapp'd my face for 't, an' so don't properly count. I be a very boastful man!"

Now I myself had felt somewhat cold inside when the guns began roaring: but this set me right in a trice. I whipp'd a pistol out of my sash and put the cold ring to his ear: and he scrambled up; and was a very lion all the rest of the day.

But now we had again to change our course, for to my dismay I saw a line of sharpshooters moving down among the gorsebushes, to take the Cornishmen in flank. And 'twas lucky we had but a little way further to go; for these skirmishers, thinking perhaps from my dress and our running thus that we bore some message open'd fire on us: and tho' they were bad marksmen, 'twas ugly to see their bullets pattering into the turf, to right and left.

We caught up the very last line of the ascending troop—lean, hungry looking men, with wan faces, but shouting lustily. I think they were about three hundred in all. "Come on, lad," called out a bearded fellow with a bandage over one eye, making room for me at his side; "there's work for plenty more!"—and a minute after, a shot took him in the ribs, and he scream'd out "Oh, my God!" and flinging up his arms, leap'd a foot in air and fell on his face.

Pressing up, I noted that the first line was now at the foot of the earthwork; and, in a minute, saw their steel caps and crimson sashes swarming up the face of it, and their pikes shining. But now came a shock, and the fellow in front was thrust back into my arms. I reeled down a pace or two and then, finding foothold, stood pushing. And next,

175

the whole body came tumbling back on me, and down the hill we went flying, with oaths and cries. Three of the rebel regiments had been flung on us and by sheer weight bore us before them. At the same time the sharpshooters pour'd in a volley: and I began to see how a man may go through a battle, and be beat, without striking a blow.

But in the midst of this scurry I heard the sound of cheering. 'Twas Sir John Berkeley's troop (till now posted under cover of the hedges below) that had come to our support; and the rebels, fearing to advance too far, must have withdrawn again behind their earthwork, for after a while the pressure eas'd a bit, and, to my amaze, the troop which but a minute since was a mere huddled crowd, formed in some order afresh, and once more began to climb. This time, I had a thick-set pikeman in front of me, with a big wen at the back of his neck that seem'd to fix all my attention. And up we went, I counting the beat of my heart that was already going hard and short with the work; and then, amid the rattle and thunder of their guns, we stopp'd again.

I had taken no notice of it, but in the confusion of the first repulse the greater part of our men had been thrust past me, so that now I found myself no further back than the fourth rank, and at the very foot of the earthwork, up the which our leaders were flung like a wave; and soon I was scrambling after them, ankle deep in the sandy earth, the man with the wen just ahead, grinding my instep with his heel and poking his pike staff between my knees as he slipp'd.

And just at the moment when the top of our wave was cleaving a small breach above us, he fell on the flat of his pike, with his nose buried in the gravel and his hands clutching. Looking up I saw a tall rebel straddling above him with musket clubb'd to beat his brains out: whom with an effort I caught by the boot; and, the bank slipping at that instant, down we all slid in a heap, a jumble of arms and legs, to the very bottom.

Before I had the sand well out of my eyes, my comrade was up and had his pike loose; and in a twinkling, the rebel was spitted through the middle and writhing. 'Twas sickening: but before I could pull out my pistol and end his pain (as I was minded), back came our front rank a-top of us again, and down they were driven like sheep, my companion catching up the dead man's musket and ammunition bag, and I followed down the slope with three stout rebels at my heels. "What will be the end of this?" thought I.

The end was, that after forty yards or so, finding the foremost close upon me, I turn'd about and let fly with my pistol at him. He spun round twice and dropp'd: which I was wondering at (the pistol being but a poor weapon for aim) when I was caught by the arm and pull'd behind a clump of bushes handy by. 'Twas the man with the wen, and by his smoking musket I knew that 'twas he had fired the shot that killed my pursuer.

"Good turn for good turn," says he: "quick with thy other pistol!"

The other two had stopped doubtfully, but at the next discharge of my pistol they turn'd tail and went up the hill again, and we were left alone. And suddenly I grew aware that my head was aching fit to split, and lay down on the turf, very sick and ill.

My comrade took no notice of this, but, going for the dead man's musket, kept loading and firing, pausing now and then for his artillery to cool, and whistling a tune that runs in my head to this day. And all the time I heard shouts and cries and the noise of musketry all around, which made me judge that the attack was going on in many places at once. When I came to myself 'twas to hear a bugle below calling again to the charge, and once more came the two troops ascending. At their head was a slight built man, bare-headed, with the sun (that was by this, high over the hill) smiting on his brown curls, and the wind blowing them. He carried a naked sword in his hand, and waved his men forward as cheerfully as though 'twere a dance and he leading out his partner.

"Who is that yonder?" asked I, sitting up and pointing.

"Bless thy innocent heart!" said my comrade, "dostn't thee know? Tis Sir Bevill."

* * * * *

'Twould be tedious to tell the whole of this long fight, which, beginning soon after sunrise, ended not till four in the afternoon, or thereabouts: and indeed of the whole my recollection is but of continual advance and repulse on that same slope. And herein may be seen the wisdom of our generals, in attacking while the main body of the enemy's horse was away: for had the Earl of Stamford possessed a sufficient force of dragoons to let slip on us at the first discomfiture, there is little doubt he might have ended the battle there and then. As it was, the horse stood out of the fray, theirs upon the summit of the hill, ours (under Col. John Digby) on the other slope, to protect the town and act as reserve.

The foot, in four parties, was disposed about the hill on all sides; to the west—as we know—under Sir John Berkeley and Sir Bevill Grenville; to the south under General Hopton and Lord Mohun; to the east under the Colonels Tom Basset and William Godolphin; while the steep side to the north was stormed by Sir Nicholas Slanning and Colonel Godolphin, with their companies. And as we had but eight small pieces of cannon and were in numbers less than one to two, all we had to do was to march up the hill in face of their fire, catch a knock on the head, may be, grin, and come on again.

But at three o'clock, we, having been for the sixth time beaten back, were panting under cover of a hedge, and Sir John Berkeley, near by, was writing on a drumhead some message to the camp, when there comes a young man on horseback, his face smear'd with dirt and dust, and rides up to him and Sir Bevill. 'Twas (I have since learn'd) to say that the powder was all spent but a barrel or two: but this only the captains knew at the time.

"Very well, then," cries Sir Bevill, leaping up gaily. "Come along, boys—we must do it this time." And, the troop forming, once more the trumpets sounded the charge, and up we went. Away along the slope we heard the other trumpeters sounding in answer, and I believe 'twas a *sursum corda!* to all of us.

Billy Pottery was ranged on my right, in the first rank, and next to me, on the other side, a giant, near seven foot high, who said his name was Anthony Payne and his business to act as body-servant to Sir Bevill. And he it was that struck up a mighty curious song in the Cornish tongue, which the rest took up with a will. Twas incredible how it put fire into them all: and Sir Bevill toss'd his hat into the air, and after him like schoolboys we pelted, straight for the masses ahead.

For now over the rampart came a company of red musketeers, and two of russet-clad pikemen, charging down on us. A moment, and we were crushed back: another, and the chant rose again. We were grappling, hand to hand, in the midst of their files.

But, good lack! What use is swordsmanship in a charge like this? The first red coat that encounter'd me I had spitted through the lung, and, carried on by the rush, he twirled me round like a windmill. In an instant I was pass'd; the giant stepping before me and clearing a space about him, using his pike as if 'twere a flail. With a wrench I tugg'd my sword out and followed. I saw Sir Bevill, a little to the left, beaten to his knee, and carried toward me. Stretching out a hand I pull'd him on his feet again, catching, as I did so, a crack on the skull that would have ended me, had not Billy Pottery put up his pike and broke the force of it. Next, I remember gripping another red coat by the beard and thrusting at him with shortened blade. Then the giant ahead lifted his pike high, and we fought to rally round it; and with that I seem'd caught off my feet and swept forward:—and we were on the crest.

Taking breath, I saw the enemy melting off the summit like a man's breath off a pane. And Sir Bevill caught my hand and pointed across to where, on the north side, a white standard embroider'd with gold griffins was mounting.

"'Tis dear Nick Slanning!" he cried; "God be prais'd—the day is ours for certain!"

CHAPTER XVII.

I MEET WITH A HAPPY ADVENTURE BY BURNING OF A GREEN LIGHT.

The rest of this signal victory (in which 1,700 prisoners were taken, besides the Major-General Chudleigh; and all the rebels' camp, cannon and victuals) I leave historians to tell. For very soon after the rout was assured (the plain below full of men screaming and running, and Col. John Digby's dragoons after them, chasing, cutting, and killing), a wet muzzle was thrust into my hand, and turning, I found Molly behind me, with the groom to whom I had given her in the morning. The rogue had counted on a crown for his readiness, and swore the mare was ready for anything, he having mix'd half a pint of strong ale with her mash, not half an hour before.

So I determin'd to see the end of it, and paying the fellow, climb'd into the saddle. On the summit the Cornish captains were now met, and cordially embracing. 'Tis very sad in these latter times to call back their shouts and boyish laughter, so soon to be quench'd on Lansdowne slopes, or by Bristol graff. Yet, O favor'd ones!—to chase Victory, to grasp her flutt'ring skirt, and so, with warm, panting cheeks, kissing her, to fall, escaping evil days!

How could they laugh? For me, the late passionate struggle left me shaken with sobs; and for the starting tears I saw neither moors around, nor sun, nor twinkling sea. Brushing them away, I was aware of Billy Pottery striding at my stirrup, and munching at a biscuit he had found in the rebels' camp. Said he, "In season, Jack, is in reason. There be times to sing an' to dance, to marry and to give in marriage; an' likewise times to become as wax: but now, lookin' about an' seein' no haughty slaughterin' cannon but has a Cornishman seated 'pon the touch-hole of the same, says I in my thoughtsome way, 'Forbear!'"

Presently he pulls up before a rebel trooper, that was writhing on the slope with a shatter'd thigh, yet raised himself on his fists to gaze on us with wide, painful eyes.

"Good sirs," gasp'd out the rebel, "can you tell me—where be Nat Shipward?"

"Now how should I know?" I answer'd.

"'A had nutty-brown curls, an' wore a red jacket—Oh, as straight a young man as ever pitched hay! 'a sarved in General Chudleigh's troop— a very singular straight young man."

"Death has taken a many such," said I, and thought on the man I had run through in our last charge.

The fellow groaned. "'A was my son," he said: and though Billy pull'd out a biscuit (his pockets bulged with them) and laid it beside him, he turn'd from it, and sank back on the turf again.

We left him, and now, the descent being gentler, broke into a run, in hopes to catch up with Col. John Digby's dragoons, that already were far across the next vale. The slope around us was piled with dead and dying, whereof four out of every five were rebels; and cruelly they cursed us as we passed them by. Night was coming on apace; and here already we were in deep shadow, but could see the yellow sun on the hills beyond. We crossed a stream at the foot, and were climbing again. Behind us the cheering yet continued, though fainter: and fainter grew the cries and shouting in front. Soon we turn'd into a lane over a steep hedge, under the which two or three stout rebels were cowering. As we came tumbling almost atop of them, they ran yelling: and we let them go in peace.

The lane gradually led us to westward, out of the main line of the rout, and past a hamlet where every door was shut and all silent. And at last a slice of the sea fronted us, between two steeply shelving hills. On the crest of the road, before it plunged down toward the coast, was a wagon lying against the hedge, with the horses gone: and beside it, stretch'd across the road, an old woman. Stopping, we found her dead, with a sword-thrust through the left breast; and inside the wagon a young man lying, with his jaw bound up,—dead also. And how this sad spectacle happened here, so far from the battlefield, was more than we could guess.

I was moving away, when Billy, that was kneeling in the road, chanced to cast his eyes up toward the sea, and dropping the dead woman's hand scrambled on his feet and stood looking, with a puzzled face.

Following his gaze, I saw a small sloop moving under shorten'd canvas, about two miles from the land. She made a pleasant sight, with the last rays of sunlight flaming on her sails: but for Billy's perturbation I could not account, so turn'd an enquiring glance to him.

"Suthin' i' the wind out yonder," was his answer: "What's a sloop doing on that ratch so close in by the point? Be dang'd! but there she goes again;"—as the little vessel swung off a point or two further from the breeze, that was breathing softly up Channel. "Time to sup, lad, for the both of us," he broke off shortly.

Indeed, I was faint with hunger by this time, yet had no stomach to eat thus close to the dead. So turning into a gate on our left hand, we cross'd two or three fields, and sat down to sup off Billy's biscuits, the mare standing quietly beside us, and cropping the short grass.

The field where we now found ourselves ran out along the top of a small promontory, and ended, without fence of any sort, at the cliff's edge. As I sat looking southward, I could only observe the sloop by turning my head: but Billy, who squatted over against me, hardly took his eyes off her, and between this and his meal was too busy to speak a word. For me, I had enough to do thinking over the late fight: and being near worn out, had half a mind to spend the night there on the hard turf: for, though the sun was now down and the landscape grey, yet the air was exceeding warm: and albeit, as I have said, there breath'd a light breeze now and then, 'twas hardly cool enough to dry the sweat off me. So I stretch'd myself out, and found it very pleasant to lie still; nor, when Billy stood up and sauntered off toward the far end of the headland, did I stir more than to turn my head and lazily watch him.

He was gone half an hour at the least, and the sky by this time was so dark, that I had lost sight of him, when, rising on my elbow to look around, I noted a curious red glow at a point where the turf broke off, not three hundred yards behind me, and a thin smoke curling up in it, as it seem'd, from the very face of the cliff below. In a minute or so the smoke ceased almost; but the shine against the sky continued steady, tho' not very strong. "Billy has lit a fire," I guessed, and was preparing to go and look, when I spied a black form crawling toward me, and presently saw 'twas Billy himself.

Coming close, he halted, put a finger to his lip and beckoned: then began to lead the way back as he had come.

Thought I, "these are queer doings:" but left Molly to browse, and crept after him on hands and knees. He turn'd his head once to make sure I was following, and then scrambled on quicker, but softly, toward the point where the red glow was shining.

Once more he pull'd up—as I judg'd, about twelve paces' distance from the edge—and after considering for a second, began to move again; only now he worked a little to the right. And soon I saw the intention of this: for just here the cliff's lip was cleft by a fissure—very like that in Scawfell which we were used to call the *Lord's Rake*, only narrower—that ran back into the field and shelved out gently at the top, so that a man might easily scramble some way down it, tho' how far I could not then tell. And 'twas from this fissure that the glow came.

Along the right lip of this Billy led me, skirting it by a couple of yards, and wriggling on his belly like a blind worm. Crawling closer now (for 'twas hard to see him against the black turf), I stopp'd beside him and strove to quiet the violence of my breathing. Then, after a minute's pause, together we pulled ourselves to the edge, and peer'd over.

The descent of the gully was broken, some eight feet below us, by a small ledge, sloping outward about six feet (as I guess), and screen'd by branches of the wild tamarisk. At the back, in an angle of the solid rock, was now set a pan pierced with holes, and full of burning charcoal: and over this a man in the rebels' uniform was stooping.

He had a small paper parcel in his left hand, and was blowing at the charcoal with all his might. Holding my breath, I heard him clearly, but could see nothing of his face, for his back was toward us, all sable against the glow. The charcoal fumes as they rose chok'd me so, that I was very near a fit of coughing, when Billy laid one hand on my shoulder, and with the other pointed out to seaward.

Looking that way, I saw a small light shining on the sea, pretty close in. 'Twas a lantern hung out from the sloop, as I concluded on the instant: and now I began to have an inkling of what was toward.

But looking down again at the man with the charcoal pan I saw a black head of hair lifted, and then a pair of red puff'd cheeks, and a pimpled nose with a scar across the bridge of it—all shining in the glare of the pan.

"Powers of Heaven!" I gasped; "'tis that bloody villain Luke Settle!"

And springing to my feet, I took a jump over the edge and came sprawling on top of him. The scoundrel was stooping with his nose close to the pan, and had not time to turn before I lit with a thud on his shoulders, flattening him on the ledge and nearly sending his face on top of the live coal. 'Twas so sudden that, before he could so much as think, my fingers were about his windpipe, and the both of us struggling flat on the brink of the precipice. For he had a bull's strength, and heaved and kicked, so that I fully looked, next moment, to be flying over the edge into the sea: nor could I loose my grip to get out a pistol, but only held on and worked my fingers in, and thought how he had strangled the mastiff that night on the bowling-green, and vowed to serve him the same if only strength held out.

But now, just as he had almost twisted his neck free, I heard a stone or two break away above us, and down came Billy Pottery flying atop of us, and pinned us to the ledge.

'Twas short work now. Within a minute, Captain Luke Settle was turned on his back, his eyes fairly starting with Billy's clutch on his throat, his mouth wide open and gasping; till I slipp'd the nozzle of my pistol between his teeth; and with that he had no more chance, but gave in, and like a lamb submitted to have his arms truss'd behind him with Billy's leathern belt, and his legs with his own.

"Now," said I, standing over him, and putting the pistol against his temple, "you and I, Master Turncoat Settle, have some accounts that 'twould be well to square. So first tell me, what do you here, and where is Mistress Delia Killigrew?"

I think that till this moment the bully had no idea his assailants were more than a chance couple of Cornish troopers. But now seeing the glow of the burning charcoal on my face, he ripped out a horrid blasphemous curse, and straightway fell to speaking calmly.

"Good sirs, the game is yours, with care. S'lid! but you hold a pretty hand—if only you know how to play it."

"'Tis you shall help me, Captain: but let us be clear about the stakes. For you, 'tis life or death: for me, 'tis to regain Mistress Delia, failing which I shoot you here through the head, and topple you into the sea. You are the Knave of trumps, sir, and I play that card: as matters now stand, only the Queen can save you."

"Right: but where be King and Ace?"

"The King is the Cornish army, yonder: the Ace is my pistol here, which I hold."

"And that's a very pretty comprehension of the game, sir: I play the Queen."

"Where is she?"

For answer, he pointed seaward, where the sloop's lantern lay like a floating star on the black waters.

"What!" cried I. "Mistress Delia in that sloop! And who is with her, pray?"

"Why, Black Dick, to begin with—and Reuben Gedges—and Jeremy Toy."

"All the Knaves left in the pack—God help her!" I muttered, as I look'd out toward the light, and my heart beat heavily. "God help her!" I said again, and turning, spied a grin on the Captain's face.

"Under Providence," answered he, "your unworthy servant may suffice. But what is my reward to be?"

"Your neck," said I, "if I can save it when you are led before the Cornish captains."

"That's fair enough: so listen. These few months the lady has been shut in Bristol keep, whither, by the advice of our employer, we conveyed her back safe and sound. This same employer—"

"A dirty rogue, whom you may as well call by his name—Hannibal Tingcomb."

"Right, young sir: a very dirty rogue, and a niggardly:—I hate a mean rascal. Well, fearing her second escape from that prison, and being hand in glove with the Parliament men, he gets her on board a sloop bound for the Virginias, just at the time when he knows the Earl of Stamford is to march and crush the Cornishmen. For escort she has the three comrades of mine that I named: and the captain of the sloop (a fellow that asks no questions) has orders to cruise along the coast hereabouts till he gets news of the battle."

"Which you were just now about to give him," cried I, suddenly enlighten'd.

"Right again. 'Twas a pretty scheme: for—d'ye see?—if all went well with the Earl of Stamford, the King's law would be wiped out in Cornwall, and Master Tingcomb (with his claims and meritorious services) might snap his thumb thereat. So, in that case, Mistress Delia was to be brought ashore here and taken to him, to serve as he fancied. But if the day should go against us—as it has—she was to sail to the Virginias with the sloop, and there be sold as a slave. Or worse might happen; but I swear that is the worst was ever told me."

"God knows 'tis vile enough," said I, scarce able to refrain from blowing his brains out. "So you were to follow the Earl's army, and work the signals. Which are they?" For a quick resolve had come into my head, and I was casting about to put it into execution.

"A green light if we won: if not, a red light, to warn the sloop away."

I picked up the packet that had dropp'd from his hand when first I sprang upon him. It was burst abroad, and a brown powder trickling from it about the ledge.

"This was the red light—to be sprinkled on the burning charcoal, I suppose?"

The fellow nodded. At the same moment, Billy (who as yet had not spoke a word, and of course, understood nothing) thrust into my hand another packet that he had found stuck in a corner against the rock.

"Now tell me—in case the rebels won, where was the landing to be made?"

"In the cove below here—where the road leads down."

"Aye, the road where the wagon stood."

Captain Luke Settle blink'd his eyes at this: but nodded after a moment.

"And how many would escort her?"

He caught my drift and laughed softly—

"Be damn'd, sir, but I begin to love you, for you play the game very proper and soundly. Reuben, Jeremy, and Black Dick alone are in the plot; so why should more escort her? For the skipper and crew have their own business to look after."

"Then, Master Settle, tho' it be a sore trial to you, those three Knaves you must give me, or I play my Ace," and I pressed the ring of my pistol sharply against his ear as a reminder.

"With all my heart, young sir, you shall have them," says he briskly.

"And this is 'honor among thieves,'" thought I: "You would sell your comrade as you sold your King:" but only said, "If you cry out, or speak one word to warn them—"

Before I could get my sentence out, Billy Pottery broke in with a voice like a trumpet—

"As folks go, Jack, I be a humorous man. But sittin' here, an' ponderin' this way an' that, I says, in my deaf an' afflicted style, 'Why not shoot the ugly rogue, if mirth, indeed, be your object?' For to wait till an uglier comes to this untravel'd spot is superfluity."

How to explain matters to Billy was more than I could tell: but in a moment he himself supplied the means. For the rocks here were of some kind of slate, very hard, but scaly: and finding two pieces, a large and a small, he handed them to me, bawling that I was to write therewith. So giving him my pistol, I made shift to scribble a few words. Seeing his eyes twinkle as he read, I stood up.

The charcoal by this time was a glowing mass of red: and threw so clear a light on us that I feared the crew on board the sloop might see our forms and suspect their misadventure. But the lantern still hung steadily: so signing to Billy to drag our prisoner behind a tamarisk bush, I open'd the second packet, and poured some of the powder into my hand.

It was composed of tiny crystals, yellow and flaky: and holding it, for a moment I was possessed with a horrid fear that this might be the signal to warn the sloop away. I flung a look at the Captain: who read my thoughts on the instant.

"Never fear, young sir: am no such hero as to sell my life for that tag-rag. Only make haste, for your deaf friend has a cursed ugly way of fumbling his pistol."

So taking heart, I tore the packet wide, and shook out the powder on the coals.

Instantly there came a dense choking vapor, and a vivid green flare that turned the rocks, the sky, and our faces to a ghastly brilliance. For two minutes, at least, this unnatural light lasted. As soon as it died away and the fumes clear'd, I look'd seaward.

The lantern on the sloop was moving in answer to the signal. Three times it was lifted and lower'd: and then in the stillness I heard voices calling, and soon after the regular splash of oars.

There was no time to be lost. Pulling the Captain to his feet, we scrambled up the gully, and out at the top, and across the fields as fast as our legs would take us. Molly came to my call and trotted beside me—the Captain following some paces behind, and Billy last, to keep a safe watch on his movements.

At the gate, however, where we turned into the road, I tethered the mare, lest the sound of her hoofs should betray us: and down toward the sea we pelted, till almost at the foot of the hill I pull'd up and listen'd, the others following my example.

We could hear the sound of oars plain above the wash of waves on the beach. I look'd about me. On either side the road was now bank'd by tall hills, with clusters of bracken and furze bushes lying darkly on their slopes. Behind one of these clusters I station'd Billy with the Captain's long sword, and a pistol that I by signs forbade him to fire unless in extremity. Then, retiring some forty paces up the road, I hid the Captain and myself on the other side.

Hardly were we thus disposed, before I heard the sound of a boat grounding on the beach below, and the murmur of voices; and then the noise of feet trampling the shingle. Upon which I ordered my prisoner to give a hail, which he did readily.

"Ahoy, Dick! Ahoy, Reuben Gedges!"

In a moment or two came the answer—

"Ahoy, there, Captain—here we be!"

"Fetch along the cargo!" shouted Captain Settle, on my prompting. "Where be you?"

"Up the road, here—waiting!"

"One minute, then—wait one minute, Captain!"

I heard the boat push'd off, some *Good-nights* call'd, and then (with tender anguish) the voice of my Delia lifted in entreaty. As I guess'd, she was beseeching the sailors to take her back to the sloop, nor leave her to these villains. There follow'd an oath or two growl'd out, a short scrimmage, and at last, above the splash of the retreating boat, came the tramp of heavy feet on the road below.

So fired was I at the sound of Delia's voice, that 'twas with much ado I kept quiet behind the bush. Yet I had wit enough left to look to the priming of my pistol, and also to bid the Captain shout again. As he did so, a light shone out down the road, and round the corner came a man bearing a lantern.

"Can't be quicker, Captain," he called: "the jade struggles so that Dick and Jeremy ha' their hands full."

Sure enough, after him there came in view two stooping forms that bore my dear maid between them—one by the feet, the other by the shoulders. I ground my teeth to see it, for she writhed sorely. On they came, however, until not more than ten paces off; and then that traitor, Luke Settle, rose up behind our bush.

"Set her here, boys," said he, "and tie her pretty ankles."

"Well met, Captain!" said the fellow with the lantern—Reuben Gedges—stepping forward; "Give us your hand!"

He was holding out his own, when I sprang up, set the pistol close to his chest, and fired. His scream mingled with the roar of it, and dropping the lantern, he threw up his hands and tumbled in a heap. At the same moment, out went the light, and the other rascals, dropping Delia, turn'd to run, crying, "Sold—sold!"

But behind them came now a shout from Billy, and a crashing blow that almost severed Black Dick's arm at the shoulder: and at the same instant I was on Master Toy's collar, and had him down in the dust. Kneeling on his chest, with my sword point at his throat, I had leisure to glance at Billy, who in the dark, seem'd to be sitting on the head of his disabled victim. And then I felt a touch on my shoulder, and a dear face peer'd into mine.

"Is it Jack—my sweet Jack?"

"To be sure," said I: "and if you but reach out your hand, I will kiss it, for all that I'm busy with this rogue."

"Nay, Jack, I'll kiss thee on the cheek—so! Dear lad, I am so frighten'd, and yet could laugh for joy!"

But now I caught the sound of galloping on the road above, and shouts, and then more galloping; and down came a troop of horsemen that were like to have ridden over us, had I not shouted lustily.

"Who, in the fiend's name is here?" shouted the foremost, pulling in his horse with a scramble.

"Honest men and rebels together," I answered; "but light the lantern that you will find handy by, and you shall know one from t'other."

By the time 'twas found and lit, there was a dozen of Col. John Digby's dragoons about us: and before the two villains were bound, comes a half dozen more, leading in Captain Settle, that had taken to his heels at the first blow and climb'd the hill, all tied as he was about the hands, and was caught in his endeavor to clamber on Molly's back. So he and Black Dick and Jeremy Toy were strapp'd up: but Reuben Gedges we left on the road for a corpse. Yet he did not die (though shot through the lung), but recovered—heaven knows how: and I myself had the pleasure to see him hanged at Tyburn, in the second year of his late Majesty's most blessed Restoration, for stopping the Bishop of Salisbury's coach, in Maidenhead Thicket, and robbing the Bishop himself, with much added contumely.

But as we were ready to start, and I was holding Delia steady on Molly's back, up comes Billy and bawls in my ear—

"There's a second horse, if wanted, that I spied tether'd under a hedge younder"—and he pointed to the field where we had first found Captain Settle—"in color a sad black, an' harness'd like as if he came from a cart."

I look'd at the Captain, who in the light of the lantern blink'd again. "Thou bloody villain!" muttered I, for now I read the tragedy of the wagon beside the road, and knew how Master Settle had provided a horse for his own escape.

But hereupon the word was given, and we started up the hill, I walking by Delia's stirrup and listening to her talk as if we had never been parted—yet with a tenderer joy, having by loss of it learn'd to appraise my happiness aright.

CHAPTER XVIII.

JOAN DOES ME HER LAST SERVICE.

We came, a little before midnight, to Sir Bevill's famous great house of Stow, near Kilkhampton: that to-night was brightly lit and full of captains and troopers feasting, as well they needed to, after the great victory. And here, though loth to do so, I left Delia to the care of Lady Grace Grenville, Sir Bevill's fond beautiful wife, and of all gentlewomen I have ever seen the pink and paragon, as well for her loyal heart as the graces of her mind: who, before the half of our tale was out, kissed Delia on both cheeks, and led her away. "To you too, sir, I would counsel bed," said she, "after you have eaten and drunk, and especially given God thanks for this day's work."

Sir Bevill I did not see, but striding down into the hall, picked my way among the drinking and drunken; the servants hurrying with dishes of roast and baked and great tankards of beer; the swords and pikes flung down under the forms and settles, and sticking out to trip a man up; and at length found a groom who led me to a loft over one of the barns: and here, above a mattress of hay, I slept the first time for many months between fresh linen that smell'd of lavender, and in thinking how pleasant 'twas, dropped sound asleep.

Sure there is no better, sweeter couch than this of linen spread over hay. Early in the morning, I woke with wits clear as water, and not an ache or ounce of weariness in my bones: and after washing at the pump below, went in search of breakfast and Sir Bevill. The one I found, ready laid, in the hall; the other seated in his writing-room, studying in a map; and with apology for my haste, handed him Master Tingcomb's confession and told my story.

When 'twas over, Sir Bevill sat pondering, and after a while said, very frankly—

"As a magistrate I can give this warrant; and 'twould be a pleasure, for well, as a boy, do I remember Deakin Killigrew. Young sir—" he rose up, and taking a turn across the room, came and laid a hand on my shoulder, "I have seen his daughter. Is it too late to warn you against loving her?"

"Why yes," I answer'd blushing: "I think it is."

"She seems both sweet and quaint. God forbid I should say a word against one that has so taken me! But in these times a man should stand alone: to make a friend is to run the chance of a soft heart: to marry a wife makes the chance sure—"

He broke off, and went on again with a change of tone—

"For many reasons I would blithely issue this warrant. But how am I to spare men to carry it out? At any moment we may be assail'd."

"If that be your concern, sir," answer'd I, "give me the warrant. I have a good friend here, a seafaring man, whose vessel lies at this moment in Looe Haven, with a crew on board that will lay Master Tingcomb by the heels in a trice. Within three days we'll have him clapp'd in Launceston Jail, and there at the next Assize you shall sit on the Grand Jury and hear his case, by which time, I hope, the King's law shall run on easier wheels in Cornwall. The prisoners we have already I leave you to deal withal: only, against my will, I must claim some mercy for that rogue, Settle."

To this Sir Bevill consented; and, to be short, the three knaves were next morning pack'd off to Launceston: but in time, no evidence being brought against them, regained their freedom, which they used to come to the gallows, each in his own way. Their doings no longer concern this history, and so I gladly leave them.

To return, then, to my proper tale, 'twas not ten minutes before I had the warrant in my pocket. And by eleven o'clock (word having been carried to Delia, and our plans laid before Billy Pottery, who on the spot engaged himself to help us) our horses were brought round to the gate, and my mistress appear'd, all ready for the journey. For tho' assured that the work needed not her presence, and that she had best wait at Stow till Master Tingcomb was smok'd out of his nest, she would have none of it, but was set on riding with me to see justice done on this fellow, of whose villainy I had told her much the night before. And glad I was of her choice, as I saw her standing on the entrance steps, fresh as a rose, and in a fit habit once more: for Lady Grace had lent not only her own bay horse, but also a riding dress and hat of grey velvet to equip her: and stood in the porch to wish us *Godspeed!* while Sir Bevill help'd Delia to the saddle.

So, with Billy tramping behind us, away we rode up the combe, where Kilkhampton tower stood against the sky; and turning to wave hands at the top, found our host and hostess still by the gate, watching us, with hands rais'd to shield their eyes from the sun.

The whole petty tale of this day's ride I shall not dwell upon. Indeed, I scarcely noted the miles as they pass'd. For all the way we were chattering, Delia telling me how Captain Settle and his gang had hurried her (tho' without indignity) across Dartmoor to Ashburton, thence to Lynton in North Devon, and so along the coast of Somerset to Bristol; how they there produced a paper, at sight of which Sir Nathaniel Fiennes, the new Governor, kept her under lock and key. And thus she remained four months, at the end of which time they convey'd her on board a sloop, call'd the *Fortitude*, and bound for the Virginias, with the result that has been told. To all of which I listened greedily, stealing from time to time a look at her shape, that on horseback was graceful as a willow, and into her eyes that, under the flapping grey brim, were gay and fancy-free as ever.

"And did you," asked I, "never at heart chide me for leaving you so!"

"Why no. I never took thee for a conjurer, Jack."

"But, at least, you thought of me," I urged.

"Oh, dear—oh, dear!" She pull'd rein and look'd at me: "I remember now that last night I kiss'd thee. Forget it, Jack: last night, so glad was I to be sav'd, I could have kiss'd a cobbler. Indeed, Jack," she went on seriously, "I would that some maid had got hold of thee, in all these months, to cure thy silly notions!"

At Launceston, Billy Pottery took leave of us: and now went, due south, toward Looe, with a light purse and lighter heart, undertaking that his ship should lie off Gleys, with her crew ready for action, within eight-and-forty hours. Delia and I rode faster now toward the southwest: and having by this time recover'd my temper, I was recounting my flight along this very road, when I heard a sound that brought my heart into my mouth.

'Twas the blast of a bugle, and came from behind the hill in front of us. And at the same moment I understood. It must be Sir George Chudleigh's cavalry returning, on news of their comrades' defeat, and we were riding straight toward them, as into a trap.

Now what could have made me forgetful of this danger I cannot explain, unless it be that our thorough victory over the rebels had given me the notion that the country behind us was clear of foes. And Sir Bevill must have had a notion we were going straight to Looe with Billy. At any rate, there was no time to be lost: for my presence was a danger to Delia as well. I cast a glance about me. There was no place to hide.

"Quick!" I cried; "follow me, and ride for dear life!"

And striking spur into Molly I turn'd sharp off the road and gallop'd across the moor to the left, with Delia close after me.

We had gone about two hundred yards only when I heard a shout, and glancing over my right shoulder, saw a green banner waving on the crest of the road, and gathered about it the vanguard of the troop—some score of dragoons: and these, having caught sight of us, were pausing a moment to watch.

196

The shout presently was followed by another; to which I made no answer, but held on my way, with the nose of Delia's horse now level with my stirrup: for I guess'd that my dress had already betrayed us. And this was the case; for at the next glance I saw five or six dragoons detach themselves from the main body, and gallop in a direction at an acute angle to ours. On they came, yelling to us to halt, and scattering over the moor to intercept us.

Not choosing, however, to be driven eastward, I kept a straight course and trusted to our horses' fleetness to carry us by them, out of reach of their shot. In the pause of their first surprise we had stolen two hundred yards more. I counted and found eight men thus in pursuit of us: and to my joy heard the bugle blown again, and saw the rest of the troop, now gathering fast above, move steadily along the road without intention to follow. Doubtless the news of the Cornish success made them thus wary of their good order.

Still, eight men were enough to run from; and now the nearest let fly with his piece—more to frighten us, belike, than with any other view, for we were far out of range. But it grew clear that if we held on our direction they must cut us off: as you may see by these two arrows, the long thin one standing for our own course, the thicker and shorter for that of the dragoons.

Only now with good hope I saw a hill rising not half a mile in front, and somewhat to the right of our course: and thought I "if we can gain the hollow to the left of it, and put the hill between us, they must ride over it or round—in either case losing much time." So, pointing this out to Delia, who rode on my left (to leave my pistol arm free and at the same time be screen'd by me from shot of the dragoons) I drove my spurs deep and called to Molly to make her best pace.

The enemy divin'd our purpose: and in a minute 'twas a desperate race for the entrance to the hollow. But our horses were the faster, and we the lighter riders; so that we won, with thirty yards to spare, from the foremost:—not without damage, however; for finding himself baulked, he sent a bullet at us which cut neatly through my off rein, so that my bridle was henceforward useless and I could guide Molly with knee and voice alone. Delia's bay had shied at the sound of it, and likely enough saved my mistress' life by this; for the bullet must have pass'd within a foot before her.

Down the hollow we raced with three dragoons at our heels, the rest going round the hill. But they did little good by so doing, for after the hollow came a broad, dismal sheet of water (by name Dozmare Pool, I have since heard) about a mile round and bank'd with black peat. Galloping along the left shore of this, we cut them off by near half a mile. But the three behind followed doggedly, though dropping back with every stride.

Beyond the pool came a green valley; and a stream flowing down it, which we jump'd easily. Glancing at Delia as she landed on the further side, I noted that her cheeks were glowing, and her eyes brimful of mirth.

"Say, Jack," she cried; "is not this better than love of women?"

"In Heaven's name," I called out, "take care!"

But 'twas too late. The green valley here melted into a treacherous bog, in the which her bay was already plunging over his fetlocks, and every moment sinking deeper.

"Throw me the rein!" I shouted, and catching the bridle close by the bit, lean'd over and tried to drag the horse forward. By this, Molly also was over hoofs in liquid mud. For a minute and more we heav'd and splashed: and all the while the dragoons, seeing our fix, were shouting and drawing nearer and nearer. But just as a brace of bullets splashed into the slough at our feet, we stagger'd to the harder slope, and were gaining on them again. So for twenty minutes along the spurs of the hills, we held on, the enemy falling back and hidden, every now and again, in the hollows—but always following: at the end of which time, Delia call'd from just behind me—

"Jack—here's a to-do: the bay is going lame!"

There was no doubt of it. I suppose he must have wrung his off hind leg in fighting through the quag. Any way, ten minutes more would see the end of his gallop. But at this moment we had won to the top of a stiff ascent: and now, looking down at our feet, I had the joyfullest surprise.

'Twas the moor of Temple spread below like a map, the low sun striking on the ruin'd huts to the left of us, on the roof of Joan's cottage, on the scar of the high road, and the sides of the tall tor above it.

"In ten minutes," said I, "we may be safe."

So down into the plain we hurried: and I thought for the first time of the loyal girl waiting in the cottage yonder; of my former ride into Temple; and (with angry shame) of the light heart with which I left it. To what had the summoning drums and trumpets led me? Where was the new life, then so carelessly prevented? But two days had gone, and here was I running to Joan for help, as a child to his mother.

Past the peat-ricks we struggled, the sheep-cotes, the straggling fences—all so familiar; cross'd the stream and rode into the yard.

"Jump down," I whisper'd: "we have time, and no more." Glancing back, I saw a couple of dragoons already coming over the heights. They had spied us.

Dismounting I ran to the cottage door and flung it open. A stream of light, flung back against the sun, blazed into my eyes.

I rubbed them and halted for a moment stock-still.

For Joan stood in front of me, dress'd in the very clothes I had worn on the day we first met—buff-coat, breeches, heavy boots, and all. Her back was toward me, and at the shoulder, where the coat had been cut away from my wound, I saw the rents all darn'd and patch'd with pack thread. In her hand was the mirror I had given her.

At the sound of my step on the threshold she turn'd with a short cry—a cry the like of which I have never heard, so full was it of choking joy. The glass dropp'd to the floor and was shatter'd. In a second her arms were about me, and so she hung on my neck, sobbing and laughing together.

"'Twas true—'twas true! Dear, dear Jack—dear Jack to come to me: hold me tighter, tighter—for my very heart is bursting!"

And behind me a shadow fell on the doorway: and there stood Delia regarding us.

"Good lad—all yesterday I swore to be strong and wait for years, if need be. Fie on womankind, to be so weak! All day I sat an' sat, an' did never a mite o' work—never set hand to a tool: an' by sunset I gave in an' went, cursing mysel', over the moor to Warleggan, to Alsie Pascoe, the wise woman—an' she taught me a charm—an' bless her, bless her, Jack, for't hath brought thee!"

"Joan," said I, hot with shame, taking her arms gently from my neck: "listen: I come because I am chased. Once more the dragooners are after me—not five minutes away. You must lend me a horse, and at once."

"Nay," said a voice in the doorway, "the horse, if lent, is for *me!*"

Joan turn'd, and the two women stood looking at each other;—the one with dark wonder, the other with cold disdainfulness—and I between them scarce lifting my eyes. Each was beautiful after her kind, as day and night: and though their looks cross'd for a full minute like drawn blades, neither had the mastery. Joan was the first to speak.

"Jack, is thy mare in the yard?"

I nodded.

"Give me thy pistols and thy cloak." She stepp'd to the window hole at the end of the kitchen, and look'd out. "Plenty o' time," she said; and pointed to the ladder leading to the loft above—"Climb up there, the both, and pull the ladder after. Is't *thou*, they want—or *she?*" pointing to Delia.

"Me chiefly they would catch, no doubt—being a man," I answer'd.

"Aye—bein' a man: the world's full o' folly. Then Jack do thou look after *her*, an' I'll look after *thee*. If the rebels leave thee in peace, make for the Jews' Kitchen and there abide me."

She flung my cloak about her, took my pistols and went out at the door. As she did so, the sun sank and a dull shadow swept over the moor.

"Joan!" I cried, for now I guess'd her purpose and was following to hinder her: but she had caught Molly's bridle and was already astride of her. "Get back!" she call'd softly; and then, "I make a better lad than wench, Jack,"—leap'd the mare through a gap in the wall, and in a moment was breasting the hill and galloping for the high road.

In less than a minute, as it seem'd, I heard a pounding of hoofs, and had barely time to follow Delia up the ladder and pull it after me, when two of the dragoons rode skurrying by the house, and pass'd on yelling. Their cries were hardly faint in the distance before there came another three.

"'A's a lost man, now, for sure," said one: "Be dang'd if 'a's not took the road back to Lan'son!'"

"How 'bout the gal?" ask'd another voice. "Here's her horse i' the yard."

"Drat the gal! Sam, go thou an' tackle her: reckon thou'rt warriors enow for one 'ooman."

The two hasten'd on: and presently I heard the one they call'd "Sam" dismounting in the yard. Now there was a window hole in the loft, facing, not on the yard, but toward the country behind; and running to it I saw that no more were following—the other three having, as I suppose, early given up the chase. Softly pulling out a loose stone or two, I widen'd this hole till I could thrust the ladder out of it. To my joy it just reach'd the ground. I bade Delia squeeze herself through and climb down.

But before she was halfway down I heard a wild screech in the kitchen below, and the voice of Sam shrieking—

"Help—help! Lord ha' mercy 'pon me—'tis a black cat—'tis a witch! The gal's no gal, but a witch!"

Laughing softly, I was descending the ladder when the fellow came round the corner screaming—with Jan Tergagle clawing at his back and spitting murderously. Delia had just time to slip aside, before he ran into the ladder and brought me flying on top of him. And there he lay and bellow'd till I tied him, and gagg'd his noise with a big stone in his mouth and his own scarf tied round it.

"Come!" I whisper'd: for Joan and her pursuers were out of sight. Catching up her long skirt, Delia follow'd me, and up the tor we panted together, nor rested till we were safe in the Jews' Kitchen.

"What think you of this for a hiding place?" ask'd I, with a laugh.

But Delia did not laugh. Instead, she faced me with blazing eyes, check'd herself and answer'd, cold as ice—

"Sir, you have done me a many favors. How I have trusted you in return it were best for you to remember, and for me to forget."

* * * * *

The dark drew on; the western star grew distinct and hung flashing over against our hiding; and still we sat there, hour after hour, silent, angry, waiting for Joan's return, Delia at the entrance of the den, chin on hand, scanning the heavens and never once turning toward me; I further inside, with my arms cross'd, raging against myself and all the world, yet with a sick'ning dread that Joan would never come back.

As the time lagg'd by, this terror grew and grew. But, as I think, about ten o'clock, I heard steps coming over the turf. I ran out. 'Twas Joan herself and leading Molly by the bridle. She walk'd as if tir'd, and leaving the mare at the entrance, follow'd me into the cave. Glancing round, I noted that Delia had slipp'd away.

"Am glad she's gone," said Joan shortly: "How many rebels pass'd this way, Jack?"

"Five, counting one that lies gagg'd and bound, down at the cottage."

"That leaves four:"—she stretch'd herself on the ground with a sigh—"four that'll never trouble thee more, lad."

"Why? how—"

202

"Listen, lad: sit down an' let me rest my head 'pon thy knee. Oh, Jack, I did it bravely! Eight good miles an' more I took the mare—by the Four—hol'd Cross, an' across the moor past Tober an' Catshole, an' over Brown Willy, an' round Roughtor to the nor'-west: an' there lies the bravest quag—oh, a black, bottomless hole!—an' into it I led them; an' there they lie, every horse, an' every mother's son, till Judgment Day."

"Dead?"

"Aye—an' the last twain wi' a bullet apiece in their skulls. Oh, rare! Dear heart—hold my head—so, atween thy hands. 'Put on his cast off duds,' said Alsie, 'an' stand afore the glass, sayin' "Come, true man!" nine-an'-ninety time.' I was mortal 'feard o' losin' count; but afore I got to fifty, I heard thy step an'—hold me closer, Jack."

"But Joan, are these men dead, say you?"

"Surely, yes. Why, lad, what be four rebels, up or down, to make this coil over? Hast never axed after *me!*"

"Joan—you are not hurt?"

In the darkness I sought her eyes, and, peering into them, drew back.

"Joan!"

"Hush, lad—bend down thy head, and let me whisper. I went too near—an' one, that was over his knees, let fly wi' his musket—an' Jack, I have but a minute or two. Hush lad, hush—there's no call! Wert never the man could ha' tam'd me—art the weaker, in a way: forgie the word, for I lov'd thee so, boy Jack!"

Her arms were drawing down my face to her: her eyes dull with pain.

"Feel, Jack—there—over my right breast. I plugg'd the wound wi' a peat turf. Pull it out, for 'tis bleeding inwards, and hurts cruelly—pull it out!"

As I hesitated, she thrust her own hand in and drew it forth, leaving the hot blood to gush.

"An' now, Jack, tighter—hold me tighter. Kiss me—oh, what brave times! Tighter, lad, an' call wi' me—'Church an' King!' Call, lad—'Church an'—'"

The warm arms loosen'd: the head sank back upon my lap.

I look'd up. There was a shadow across the entrance, blotting out the star of night. 'Twas Delia, leaning there and listening.

CHAPTER XIX.

THE ADVENTURE OF THE HEARSE.

The day-spring came at last, and in the sick light of it I went down to the cottage for spade and pickaxe. In the tumult of my senses I hardly noted that our prisoner, the dragoon, had contrived to slip his bonds and steal off in the night.

And then Delia, seeing me return with the sad tools on my shoulder, spoke for the first time:

"First, if there be a well near, fetch me two buckets of water, and leave us for an hour."

Her voice was weary and chill: so that I dared not thank her, but did the errand in silence. Then, but a dozen paces from the spot where Joan's father lay, I dug a grave and strew'd it with bracken, and heather, and gorse petals, that in the morning air smell'd rarely. And soon after my task was done, Delia call'd me.

In her man's dress Joan lay, her arms cross'd, her black tresses braided, and her face gentler than ever 'twas in life. Over her wounded breast was a bunch of some tiny pink flower, that grew about the tor.

So I lifted her softly as once in this same place she had lifted me, and bore her down the slope to the grave: and there I buried her, while Delia knelt and pray'd, and Molly browsed, lifting now and then her head to look.

When all was done, we turn'd away, dry-eyed, and walked together to the cottage. The bay horse was feeding on the moor below; and finding him still too lame to carry Delia, I shifted the saddles, and mending the broken rein, set her on Molly. The cottage door stood open, but we did not enter; only look'd in, and seeing Jan Tergagle curl'd beside the cold hearth, left him so.

Mile after mile we pass'd in silence, Delia riding, and I pacing beside her with the bay. At last, tortur'd past bearing, I spoke—

"Delia, have you nothing to say?"

For a while she seem'd to consider: then, with her eyes fix'd on the hills ahead, answered—

"Much, if I could speak: but all this has changed me somehow—'tis, perhaps, that I have grown a woman, having been a girl—and need to get used to it, and think."

She spoke not angrily, as I look'd for; but with a painful slowness that was less hopeful.

"But," said I, "over and over you have shown that I am nought to you. Surely—"

"Surely I am jealous? 'Tis possible—yes, Jack, I am but a woman, and so 'tis certain."

"Why, to be jealous, you must love me!"

She look'd at me straight, and answered very deliberate—

"Now that is what I am far from sure of."

"But, dear Delia, when your anger has cool'd—"

"My anger was brief: I am disappointed, rather. With her last breath, almost, Joan said you were weaker than she: she lov'd you better than I, and read you clearer. You *are* weak. Jack"—she drew in Molly, and let her hand fall on my shoulder very kindly—"we have been comrades for many a long mile, and I hope are honest good friends; wherefore I loathe to say a harsh or ungrateful-seeming word. But you could not understand that brave girl, and you cannot understand me: for as yet you do not even know yourself. The knowledge comes slowly to a man, I think; to a woman at one rush. But when it comes, I believe you may be strong. Now leave me to think, for my head is all of a tangle."

Our pace was so slow (by reason of the lame horse), that a great part of the afternoon was spent before we came in sight of the House of Gleys. And truly the yellow sunshine bad flung some warmth about the naked walls and turrets, so that Delia's home-coming seem'd not altogether cheerless. But what gave us more happiness was to spy, on the blue water beyond, the bright canvas of the *Godsend*, and to hear the cries and stir of Billy Pottery's mariners as they haul'd down the sails.

And Billy himself was on the lookout with his spyglass. For hardly were we come to the beach when our signal—the waving of a white kerchief—was answered by another on board; and within half an hour a boat puts off, wherein, as she drew nearer, I counted eight fellows.

They were (besides Billy), Matt. Soames, the master, Gabriel Hutchins, Ned Masters, the black man Sampson, Ben Halliday, and two whose full names I have forgot—but one was call'd Nicholas. And, after many warm greetings, the boat was made fast, and we climbed up along the peninsula together, in close order, like a little army.

All this time there was no sign or sound about the House of Gleys to show that anyone mark'd us or noted our movements. The gate was closed, the windows stood shutter'd, as on my former visit: even the chimneys were smokeless. Such effect had this desolation on our spirits, that drawing near, we fell to speaking in whispers, and said Ned Masters—

"Now a man would think us come to bury somebody!"

"He might make a worse guess," I answer'd.

Marching up to the gate, I rang a loud peal on the bell; and to my astonishment, before the echoes had time to die away, the grating was push'd back, and the key turn'd in the lock.

"Step ye in—step ye in, good folks! A sorry day,—a day of sobs an' tears an' afflicted blowings of the nose—when the grasshopper is a burden an' the mourners go about seeking whom they may devour the funeral meats. Y' are welcome, gentlemen."

'Twas the voice of my one-eyed friend, as he undid the bolts; and now he stood in the gateway with a prodigious black sash across his canary livery, so long that the ends of it swept the flagstones.

"Is Master Tingcomb within?" I helped Delia to dismount, and gave our two horses to a stable boy that stood shuffling some paces off.

"Alas!" the old man heav'd a deep sigh, and with that began to hobble across the yard. We troop'd after, wondering. At the house door he turn'd—

"Sirs, there is cold roasted capons, an' a ham, an' radishes in choice profusion for such as be not troubled wi' the wind: an' cordial wines—alack the day!"

He squeez'd a frosty tear from his one eye, and led us to a large bare hall, hung round with portraits; where was a table spread with a plenty of victuals, and horn-handled knives and forks laid beside plates of pewter; and at the table a man in black, eating. He had straight hair and a sallow face; and look'd up as we enter'd, but, groaning, in a moment fell to again.

"Eat, sirs," the old servitor exhorted us: "alas! that man may take nothing out o' the world!"

I know not who of us was most taken aback. But noting Delia's sad wondering face, as her eyes wander'd round the neglected room and rested on the tatter'd portraits, I lost patience.

"Our business is with Master Hannibal Tingcomb," said I sharply.

The straight-hair'd man look'd up again, his mouth full of ham.

"Hush!"—he held his fork up, and shook his head sorrowfully: and I wonder'd where I had Been him before. "Hast thou an angel's wings?" he ask'd.

"Why, no, sir; but the devil's own boots—as you shall find if I be not answer'd."

"Young man—young man," broke in the one-eyed butler: "our minister is a good minister, an' speaks roundabout as such: but the short is, that my master is dead, an' in his coffin."

"The mortal part," corrected the minister, cutting another slice.

"Aye, the immortal is a-trippin' it i' the New Jeroosalem: but the mortal was very lamentably took wi' a fit, three days back—the same day, young man, as thou earnest wi' thy bloody threats."

"A fit?"

"Aye, sir, an' verily—such a fit as thou thysel' witness'd. 'Twas the third attack—an' he cried, 'Oh!' he did, an' 'Ah!'—just like that. 'Oh!' an' then 'Ah!' Such were his last dyin' speech. 'Dear Master,' says I, 'there's no call to die so hard:' but might so well ha' whistled, for he was dead as nails. A beautiful corpse, sirs, dang my buttons!"

"Show him to us."

"Willingly, young man." He led the way to the very room where Master Tingcomb and I had held our interview. As before, six candles were burning there: but the table was push'd into a corner, and now their light fell on a long black coffin, resting on trestles in the centre of the room. The coffin was clos'd, and studded with silver nails; on the lid was a silver plate bearing these words written—*"Hannibal Tingcomb*, MDCXLIIL," with a text of Scripture below.

"Why have you nail'd him down?" I asked.

"Now where be thy bowels, young man, to talk so unfeelin'? An' where be thy experience, not to know the ways o' thy blessed dead in summer time?"

"When do you bury him?"

"To-morrow forenoon. The spot is two mile from here." He blinked at me, and hesitated for a minute. "Is it your purpose, sirs, to attend?"

"Be sure of that," I said grimly. "So have beds ready to-night for all our company."

"All thy—! Dear sir, consider: where are beds to be found? Sure, thy mariners can pass the night aboard their own ship?"

"So then," thought I, "you have been on the lookout;" but Delia replied for me—

"I am Delia Killigrew, and mistress of this house. You will prepare the beds as you are told." Whereupon what does that decrepit old sinner but drop upon his knees?

"Mistress Delia! O goodly feast for this one poor eye! Oh, that Master Tingcomb had seen this day!"

I declare the tears were running down his nose; but Delia march'd out, cutting short his hypocrisy.

In the passage she whisper'd—

"Villainy, Jack!"

"Hush!" I answered, "and listen: *Master Tingcomb is no more in that coffin than I.*"

"Then where is he?"

"That is just what we are to discover." As I said this a light broke on me. "By the Lord," I cried, "'tis the very same!"

Delia open'd her eyes wide.

"Wait," I said: "I begin to touch ground."

We returned to the great hall. The straight-hair'd man was still eating, and opposite sat Billy, that had not budg'd, but now beckoning to me, very mysterious, whisper'd in a voice that made the plates rattle—

"That's—a damned—rogue!"

'Twas discomposing, but the truth. In fact, I had just solv'd a puzzle. This holy-speaking minister was no other than the groom I had seen at Bodmin Fair holding Master Tingcomb's horses.

By this, the sun was down, and Delia soon made an excuse to withdraw to her own room. Nor was it long before the rest followed her example. I found our chambers prepared, near together, in a wing of the house at some distance from the hall. Delia's was next to mine, as I made sure by knocking at her door: and on the other side of me slept Billy with two of his crew. My own bed was in a great room sparely furnish'd; and the linen indifferent white. There was a plenty of clean straw, tho', on the floor, had I intended to sleep—which I did not.

Instead, having blown out my light, I sat on the bed's edge, listening to the big clock over the hall as it chim'd the quarters, and waiting till the fellows below should be at their ease. That Master Tingcomb rested under the coffin lid, I did not believe, in spite of the terrifying fit that I could vouch for. But this, if driven to it, we could discover at the grave. The main business was to catch him; and to this end I meant to patrol the buildings, and especially watch the entrance, on the likely chance of his creeping back to the house (if not already inside), to confer with his fellow-rascals.

As eleven o'clock sounded, therefore, I tapp'd on Billy's wall; and finding that Matt. Soames was keeping watch (as we had agreed upon), slipp'd off my boots. Our rooms were on the first floor, over a straw yard; and the distance to the ground an easy drop for a man. But wishing to be silent as possible, I knotted two blankets together, and strapping the end round the window mullion, swung myself down by one hand, holding my boots in the other.

I dropp'd very lightly, and look'd about. There was a faint moon up and glimmering on the straw; but under the house was deep shadow, and along this I crept. The straw yard led into the court before the stables, and so into the main court. All this way I heard no sound, nor spied so much as a speck of light in any window. The house door was clos'd, and the bar fastened on the great gate across the yard. I turn'd the corner to explore the third side of the house.

Here was a group of outbuildings jutting out, and between them and the high outer wall a narrow alley. 'Twas with difficulty I groped my way here, for the passage was dark as pitch, and rendered the straiter by a line of ragged laurels planted under the house; so that at every other step I would stumble, and run my head into a bush.

I had done this for the eighth time, and was cursing under my breath, when on a sudden I heard a stealthy footfall coming down the alley behind me.

"Master Tingcomb, for a crown!" thought I, and crouch'd to one side under a bush. The footsteps drew nearer. A dark form parted the laurels: another moment, and I had it by the throat.

"Uugh—ugh—grr! For the Lord's sake, sir,—"

I loos'd my hold: 'twas Matt. Soames. "Your pardon," whisper'd I; "but why have you left your post?"

"Black Sampson is watchin', so I took the freedom—ugh! my poor windpipe!—to—"

He broke off to catch me by the sleeve and pull me down behind the bush. About twelve paces ahead I heard a door softly open'd and saw a shaft of light flung across the path between the glist'ning laurels. As the ray touch'd the outer wall, I mark'd a small postern gate there, standing open.

Cowering lower, we waited while a man might count fifty. Then came footsteps crunching the gravel, and a couple of men cross'd the path, bearing a large chest between them. In the light I saw the handle of a spade sticking out from it: and by his gait I knew the second man to be my one-ey'd friend.

"Woe's my old bones!" he was muttering: "here's a fardel for a man o' my years!"

"Hold thy breath for the next load!" growl'd the other voice, which as surely was the good minister's.

They pass'd out of the small gate, and by the sounds that follow'd, we guess'd they were hoisting their burden into a cart. Presently they re-cross'd the path, and entered the house, shutting the door after them.

"Now for it!" said I in Matt's ear. Gliding forward, I peep'd out at the postern gate; but drew back like a shot.

I had almost run my head into a great black hearse, that stood there with the door open, back'd against the gate, the heavy plumes nodding above it in the night wind.

Who held the horses I had not time to see: but whispering to Matt, to give me a leg up, clamber'd inside. "Quick!" I pull'd him after, and crept forward. I wonder'd the man did not hear us: but by good luck the horses were restive, and by his maudlin talk to them I knew he was three parts drunk—on the funeral wines, doubtless.

I crept along, and found the tool chest stow'd against the further end: so, pulling it gently out, we got behind it. Tho' Matt was the littlest man of my acquaintance, 'twas the work of the world to stow ourselves in such compass as to be hidden. By coiling up our limbs we managed it; but only just before I caught the glimmer of a light and heard the pair of rascals returning.

They came very slow, grumbling all the way; and of course, I knew they carried the coffin.

"All right, Sim?" ask'd the minister.

"Aye," piped a squeaky voice by the horses heads ('twas the shuffling stable boy), "aye, but look sharp! Lord, what sounds I've heerd! The devil's i' the hearse, for sure!"

"Now, Simmy," the one-ey'd gaffer expostulated, "thou dostn' think the smoky King is a-took in, same as they poor folks upstairs? Tee-hee! Lord, what a trick!—to come for Master Tingcomb, an' find—aw dear!— aw, bless my old ribs, what a thing is humor!"

"Shut up!" grunted the minister. The end of the coffin was tilted up into the hearse. "Push, old varmint!"

"Aye-push, push! Where be my young, active sinews? What a shrivell'd garment is all my comeliness! 'The devil inside,' says Simmy—haw, haw!"

"Burn the thing! 'twon't go in for the tool box. Push, thou cackling old worms!"

"Now so I be, but my natural strength is abated. 'Yo-heave ho!' like the salted seafardingers upstairs. Push, push!"

"Oh, my inwards!" groans poor Matt, under his breath, into whom the chest was squeezing sorely.

"Right at last!" says the minister. "Now, Simmy, nay lad, hand the reins an' jump up. There's room, an' you'll be wanted."

The door was clapp'd-to, the three rogues climb'd upon the seat in front: and we started.

I hope I may never be call'd to pass such another half hour as that which follow'd. As soon as the wheels left turf for the hard road, 'twas jolt, jolt all the way; and this lying mainly down hill, the chest and coffin came grinding into our ribs, and pressing till we could scarce breathe. And I dared not climb out over them, for fear the fellows should hear us; their chuckling voices coming quite plain to us from the other side of the panel. I held out, and comforted Matt, as well as I could, feeling sure we should find Master Tingcomb at our journey's end. Soon we climb'd a hill, which eas'd us a little; but shortly after were bumping down again, and suffering worse than ever.

"Save us," moan'd Matt, "where will this end?"

The words were scarce out, when we turn'd sharp to the right, with a jolt that shook our teeth together, roll'd for a little while over smooth grass, and drew up.

I heard the fellows climbing down, and got my pistols out.

"Simmy," growl'd the minister, "where's the lantern?"

There was a minute or so of silence, and then the snapping of flint and steel, and the sound of puffing.

"Lit, Simmy?"

"Aye, here 'tis."

"Fetch it along then."

The handle of the door was turn'd, and a light flash'd into the hearse.

"Here, hold the lantern steady! Come hither, old Squeaks, and help wi' the end."

"Surely I will. Well was I call'd Young Look-alive when a gay, fleeting boy. Simmy, my son, thou'rt sadly drunken. O youth, youth! Thou winebibber, hold the light steady, or I'll tell thy mammy!"

"Oh, sir, I do mortally dread the devil an' all his works!"

214

"Now, if ever! The devil,' says he—an' Master Tingcomb still livin', an' in his own house awaitin' us!"

Be sure, his words were as good as a slap in the face to me. For I had counted the hearse to lead me straight to Master Tingcomb himself. "In his own house," too! A fright seiz'd me for Delia. But first I must deal with these scoundrels, who already were dragging out the coffin.

"Steady there!" calls the minister. The coffin was more than halfway outside. I levell'd my pistol over the edge of the tool chest, and fetch'd a yell fit to wake a ghost—at the same time letting fly straight for the minister.

In the flash of the discharge, I saw him, half-turn'd, his eyes starting, and mouth agape. He clapp'd his hand to his shoulder. On top of his wild shriek, broke out a chorus of screams and oaths, in the middle of which the coffin tilted up and went over with a crash. "Satan—Satan!" bawled Simmy, and, dropping the lantern, took to his heels for dear life. At the same moment the horses took fright; and before I could scramble out, we were tearing madly away over the turf and into the darkness. I had made a sad mess of it.

It must have been a full minute before the hedge turn'd them, and gave me time to drop out at the back and run to their heads. Matt. Soames was after me, quick as thought, and very soon we mastered them, and gathering up the reins from between their legs, led them back. As luck would have it, the lantern had not been quench'd by the fall, but lay flaring, and so guided us. Also a curious bright radiance seem'd growing on the sky, for which I could not account. The three knaves were nowhere to be seen, but I heard their footsteps scampering in the distance, and Simmy still yelling "Satan!" I knew my bullet had hit the minister; but he had got away, and I never set eyes on any of the three again.

Leaving Matt to mind the horses, I caught up the lantern, and look'd about me. As well as could be seen, we were in a narrow meadow between two hills, whereof the black slopes rose high above us. Some paces to the right, my ear caught the noise of a stream running.

I turn'd the lantern on the coffin, which lay face downward, and with a gasp took in the game those precious rogues had been playing. For, with the fall of it, the boards (being but thin) were burst clean asunder; and on both sides had tumbled out silver cups, silver saltcellars, silver plates and dishes, that in the lantern's rays sparkled prettily on the turf. The coffin, in short, was stuff'd with Delia's silverware.

I had pick'd up a great flagon, and was turning it over to read the inscription, when Matt. Soames call'd to me, and pointed over the hill in front. Above it the whole sky was red and glowing.

"Sure," said he, "'tis a fire out yonder!"

"God help us, Matt.—'tis the House of Gleys!"

It took but two minutes to toss the silver back into the hearse. I clapp'd-to the door, and snatching the reins, sprang upon the driver's seat.

CHAPTER XX.

THE ADVENTURE OF THE LEDGE;
AND HOW I SHOOK HANDS WITH
MY COMRADE.

We had some ado to find the gate: but no sooner were through, and upon the high road, than I lash'd the horses up the hill at a gallop. To guide us between the dark hedges we had only our lantern and the glare ahead. The dishes and cups clash'd and rattled as the hearse bump'd in the ruts, swaying wildly: a dozen times Matt, was near being pitch'd clean out of his seat. With my legs planted firm, I flogg'd away like a madman; and like mad creatures the horses tore upward.

On the summit a glance show'd us all—the wild crimson'd sky—the sea running with lines of fire—and against it the inky headland whereon the House of Gleys flar'd like a beacon. Already from one wing—*our* wing—a leaping column of flame whirl'd up through the roof, and was swept seaward in smoke and sparks. I mark'd the coast line, the cliff tracks, the masts and hull of the *Godsend* standing out, clear as day; and nearer, the yellow light flickering over the fields of young corn. We saw all this, and then were plunging down hill, with the blaze full ahead of us. The heavy reek of it was flung in our nostrils as we gallop'd.

At the bottom we caught up a group of men running. 'Twas a boatload come from the ship to help. As our horses swept past them, one or two came to a terrified halt; but presently were running hard again after us.

The great gate stood open. I drove straight into the bright-lit yard, shouting "Delia!—where is Delia?"

"Here!" call'd a voice; and from a group that stood under the glare of the window came my dear mistress running.

"All safe, Jack! But what—" She drew back from our strange equipage.

"All in good time. First tell me—how came the fire?"

"Why, foul work, as it seems. All I know is I was sleeping, and awoke to hear the black seaman hammering on my door. Jumping up, I found the room full of smoke, and escap'd. The rooms beneath, they say, were stuff'd with straw, and the yard outside heap'd also with straw, and blazing. Ben Halliday found two oil jars lying there—"

"Are the horses out?"

"Oh, Jack—I do not know! Shame on me to forget them!"

I ran toward the stable. Already the roof was ablaze, and the straw yard, beyond, a very furnace. Rushing in, I found the two horses cowering in their stalls, bath'd in sweat, and squealing. But 'twas all fright. So I fetch'd Molly's saddle, and spoke to her, and set it across her back: and the sweet thing was quiet in a moment, turning her head to rub my sleeve gently with her muzzle: and followed me out like a lamb. The bay gave more trouble; but I sooth'd him in the same manner, and patting his neck, led him, too, into safety.

By this, all hope to save the house was over: for the well in the court yielded but twenty buckets before it ran dry, and after that no water was to be had. Of the wing where the fire burst out only the walls stood, and a few oaken rafters, that one by one came tumbling and crashing. The flames had spread along the roof, and were now licking the ceiling of the hall and spouting around the clock tower. In the roar and hubbub, Billy's men work'd like demons, dragging out chairs, chests, and furniture of all kinds, which they strew'd in the yard, returning with shouts for more. One was tearing down the portraits in the hall: another was pulling out the great dresser from the kitchen: a third had found a pile of tapestry and came staggering forth under the load of it.

I had fasten'd the horses by the gate, and was ready to join in the work, when a shout was rais'd—

"Billy!—Where's Billy Pottery? Has any seen the skipper?"

"Sure," I call'd, "you don't say he was never alarm'd!"

"Black Sampson was in his room—where's Black Sampson?"

"Here I be!" cried a voice. "To be sure I woke the skipper before any o' ye."

"Then where's he hid? Did any see him come out?"

"Now, that we have not!" answer'd one or two.

I stood by the house door shouting these questions to the men inside, when a hand was laid on my arm, and there in the shadow waited Billy himself, with a mighty curious twinkle in his eye. He put a finger up and signed that I should follow.

We pass'd round the outbuildings where, three hours before, Matt. Soames and I had hid together. I was minded to stop and pull on my boots, that were hid here: but (and this was afterward the saving of me) on second thoughts let them lie, and follow'd Billy, who now led me out by the postern gate.

Without speech we stepp'd across the turf, he a pace or two ahead. A night breeze was blowing here, delicious after the heat of the fire. We were walking quickly toward the east side of the headland, and soon the blaze behind flung our shadows right to the cliff's edge, for which Billy made straight, as if to fling himself over.

But when, at the very verge, he pull'd up, I became enlighten'd. At our feet was an iron bar driven into the soil, and to it a stout rope knotted, that ran over a block and disappeared down the cliff. I knelt and, pulling at it softly, look'd up. It came easy in the hand.

Billy, with the glare in his face, nodded: and bending to my ear, for once achiev'd a whisper.

"Saw one stealing hither—an' follow'd. A man wi' a limp foot—went over the side like a cat."

I must have appeared to doubt this good fortune, for he added—

"'Be a truth speakin' man i' the main, Jack—' lay over 'pon my belly, and spied a ledge—fifty feet down or less—' reckon there be a way thence to the foot. Dear, now! what a rampin', tearin' sweat is this?"

For, fast as I could tug, I was hauling up the rope. Near sixty feet came up before I reach'd the end—a thick twisted knot. I rove a long noose; pull'd it over my head and shoulders, and made Billy understand he was to lower me.

"Sit i' the noose, lad, an' hold round the knot. For sign to hoist again, tug the rope hard. I can hold."

He paid it out carefully while I stepp'd to the edge. With the noose about my loins I thrust myself gently over, and in a trice hung swaying.

On three sides the sky compass'd me—wild and red, save where to eastward the dawn was paling: on the fourth the dark rocky face seem'd gliding upward as Billy lower'd. Far below I heard the wash of the sea, and could just spy the white spume of it glimmering. It stole some of the heart out of me, and I took my eyes off it.

Some feet below the top, the cliff fetch'd a slant inward, so that I dangled a full three feet out from the face. As a boy I had adventured something of this sort on the north sides of Gable and the Pillar, and once (after a nest of eaglets) on the Mickledore cliffs: but then 'twas daylight. Now, tho' I saw the ledge under me, about a third of the way down, it look'd, in the darkness, to be so extremely narrow, that 'tis probable I should have call'd out to Billy to draw me up but for the certainty that he would never hear: so instead I held very tight and wish'd it over.

Down I sway'd (Billy letting out the rope very steady), and at last swung myself inward to the ledge, gain'd a footing, and took a glance round before slipping off the rope.

I stood on a shelf of sandy rock that wound round the cliff some way to my left, and then, as I thought, broke sharply away. 'Twas mainly about a yard in width, but in places no more than two feet. In the growing light I noted the face of the headland ribb'd with several of these ledges, of varying length, but all hollow'd away underneath (as I suppose by the sea in former ages), so that the cliff's summit overhung the base by a great way: and peering over I saw the waves creeping right beneath me.

Now all this while I had not let Master Tingcomb out of my mind. So I slipp'd off the rope and left it to dangle, while I crept forward to explore, keeping well against the rock and planting my feet with great caution.

I believe I was twenty minutes taking as many steps, when at the point where the ledge broke off I saw the ends of an iron ladder sticking up, and close beside it a great hole in the rock, which till now the curve of the cliff had hid. The ladder no doubt stood on a second shelf below.

I was pausing to consider this, when a bright ray stream'd across the sea toward me, and the red rim of the sun rose out of the waters, outfacing the glow on the headland, and rending the film of smoke that hung like a curtain about the horizon. 'Twas as if by alchemy that the red ripples melted to gold; and I stood watching with a child's delight.

I heard the sound of a footstep: and fac'd round.

Before me, not six paces off, stood Hannibal Tingcomb.

He was issuing from the hole with a sack on his shoulder, and sneaking to descend the steps, when he threw a glance behind—and saw me!

Neither spoke. With a face grey as ashes he turn'd very slowly, until in the unnatural light we look'd straight into each other's eyes. His never blink'd, but stared—stared horribly, while the veins swell'd black on his forehead and his lips work'd, attempting speech. No words came—only a long drawn sob, deep down in his throat.

And then, letting slip the sack, he flung his arms up, ran a pace or two toward me, and tumbled on his face in a fit. His left shoulder hung over the verge; his legs slipp'd. In a trice he was hanging by his arms, his old distorted face turn'd up, and a froth about his lips. I made a step to save him: and then jump'd back, flattening myself against the rock.

The ledge was breaking.

I saw a seam gape at my feet. I saw it widen and spread to right and left. I heard a ripping, rending noise—a rush of stones and earth: and, clawing the air, with a wild screech, Master Tingcomb pitch'd backward, head over heels, into space.

Then follow'd silence: then a horrible splash as he struck the water, far below: then again a slipping and trickling, as more of the ledge broke away—at first a pebble or two sliding—a dribble of earth—next, a crash and a cloud of dust. A last stone ran loose and dropp'd. Then fell a silence so deep I could catch the roar of the flames on the hill behind.

Standing there, my arms thrown back and fingers spread against the rock, I saw a wave run out, widen, and lose itself on the face of the sea. Under my feet but eight inches of the cornice remain'd. My toes stuck forward over the gulf.

A score of startled gulls with their cries call'd me to myself. I open'd my eyes, that had shut in sheer giddiness. Close on my left the ledge was broke back to the very base, cutting me off by twelve feet from that part where the ladder still rested. No man could jump it, standing. To the right there was no gap: but in one place only was the footing over ten inches wide, and at the end my rope hung over the sea, a good yard away from the edge.

I shut my eyes and shouted.

There was no answer. In the dead stillness I could hear the rafters falling in the House of Gleys, and the shouts of the men at work. The *Godsend* lay around the point, out of sight. And Billy, deaf as a stone, sat no doubt by his rope, placidly waiting my signal.

I scream'd again and again. The rock flung my voice seaward. Across the summit vaulted above, there drifted a puff of brown smoke. No one heard.

A while of weakness followed. My brain reel'd: my fingers dug into the rock behind till they bled. I bent forward—forward over the heaving mist through which the sea crawl'd like a snake. It beckon'd me down, that crawling water . . .

I stiffened my knees and the faintness pass'd. I must not look down again. It flashed on me that Delia had call'd me weak: and I hardened my heart to fight it out. I would face round to the cliff and work toward the rope.

'Twas a hateful moment while I turned: for to do so I must let go with one hand. And the rock thrust me outward. But at last I faced the cliff; waited a moment while my knees shook; and moving a foot cautiously to the left, began to work my way along, an inch at a time.

Looking down to guide my feet, I saw the waves twinkling beneath my heels. My palms press'd the rock. At every three inches I was fain to rest my forehead against it and gasp. Minute after minute went by—endless, intolerable, and still the rope seem'd as far away as ever. A cold sweat ran off me: a nausea possessed me. Once, where the ledge was widest, I sank on one knee, and hung for a while incapable of movement. But a black horror drove me on: and after the first dizzy stupor my wits were mercifully wide awake. Sure, 'twas God's miracle preserv'd them to me, who looking at the sea and cliff and pitiless sun, had almost denied Him and his miracles together.

All the way I kept shouting: and so, for half an hour, inch by inch, shuffled forward, until I stood under the rope. Then I had to turn again.

The rock, tho' still overarching, here press'd out less than before: so that, working round on the ball of my foot, I managed pretty easily. But how to get the rope? As I said, it hung a good yard beyond the ledge, the noose dangling some two feet below it. With my finger tips against the cliff, I lean'd out and clutch'd at it. I miss'd it by a foot. "Shall I jump?" thought I, "or bide here till help comes?"

'Twas a giddy, awful leap. But the black horror was at my heels now. In a minute more 'twould have me; and then my fall was certain. I call'd up Delia's face as she had taunted me. I bent my knees, and, leaving my hold of the rock, sprang forward—out, over the sea.

I saw it twinkle, fathoms below. My right hand touch'd—grasp'd the rope: then my left, as I swung far out upon it. I slipp'd an inch—three inches—then held, swaying wildly. My foot was in the noose. I heard a shout above: and, as I dropp'd to a sitting posture, the rope began to rise.

"Quick! Oh, Billy, pull quick!"

He could not hear; yet tugg'd like a Trojan.

"Now, here's a time to keep a man sittin'!" he shouted, as he caught my hand, and pull'd me full length on the turf. "Why, lad—hast seen a ghost?"

There was no answer. The black horror had overtaken me at last.

* * * * *

They carried me to a shed in the great court of Gleys, and set me on straw: and there, till far into the afternoon, I lay betwixt swooning and trembling, while Delia bath'd my head in water from the sea, for no other was to be had. And about four in the afternoon the horror left me, so that I sat up and told my story pretty steadily.

"What of the house?" I ask'd, when the tale was done, and a company sent to search the east cliff from the beach.

"All perish'd!" said Delia, and then smiling, "I am houseless as ever, Jack."

"And have the same good friends."

"That's true. But listen—for while you have lain here, Billy and I have put our heads together. He is bound for Brest, he says, and has agreed to take me and such poor chattels as are saved, to Brittany, where I know my mother's kin will have a welcome for me, until these troubles be pass'd. Already the half of my goods is aboard the *Godsend*, and a letter writ to

Sir Bevill, begging him to appoint an honest man as my steward. What think you of the plan?"

"It seems a good plan," I answer'd slowly: "the England that now is, is no place for a woman. When do you sail?"

"As soon as you are recovered, Jack."

"Then that's now." I got on my feet, and drew on my boots (that Matt. Soames had found in the laurel bushes and brought). My knees trembled a bit, but nothing to matter.

"Art looking downcast, Jack."

Said I: "How else should I look, that am to lose thee in an hour or more?"

She made no reply to this, but turned away to give an order to the sailors.

The last of Delia's furniture was hardly aboard, when we heard great shouts of joy, and saw the men returning that had gone to search the cliff. They bore between them three large oak coffers: which being broke, we came on an immense deal of old plate and jewels, besides over L300 in coined money. There were two more left behind, they said, besides several small bags of gold. The path up the cliff was hard to climb, and would have been impossible, but for the iron ladder they found ready fix'd for Master Tingcomb's descent. In the hole (that could not be seen from the beach, the shelf hiding it) was tackle for lowering the chest: and below a boat moor'd, and now left high and dry by the tide. Doubtless, the arch-rascal had waited for his comrades to return, whom Matt. Soames and I had scar'd out of all stomach to do so. His body was nowhere found.

The sea had wash'd it off: but the sack they recover'd, and found to hold the choicest of Delia's heirlooms. Within an hour the remaining coffers and the money bags were safe in the vessel's hold.

* * * * *

The sun was setting, as Delia and I stood on the beach, beside the boat that was to take her from me. Aboard the *Godsend* I could hear the anchor lifting, and the men singing, as, holding Molly's bridle, I held out my hand to the dear maid who with me had shar'd so many a peril.

"Is there any more to come?" she ask'd.

"No," said I, and God knows my heart was heavy: "nothing to come but 'Farewell!'"

She laid her small hand in my big palm, and glancing up, said very pretty and demur—

"And shall I leave my best? Wilt not come, too, dear Jack?"

"Delia!" I stammer'd. "What is this? I thought you lov'd me not."

"And so did I, Jack: and thinking so, I found I loved thee better than ever. Fie on thee, now! May not a maid change her mind without being forced to such unseemly, brazen words?" And she heav'd a mock sigh.

But as I stood and held that little hand, I seem'd across the very mist of happiness to read a sentence written, and spoke it, perforce and slow, as with another man's mouth—

"Delia, you only have I lov'd, and will love! Blithe would I be to live with you, and to serve you would blithely die. In sorrow, then, call for me, or in trust abide me. But go with you now—I may not."

She lifted her eyes, and looking full into mine, repeated slowly the verse we had read at our first meeting—

> "'In a wife's lap, as in a grave,
> Man's airy notions mix with earth—'

—thou hast found it, sweetheart—thou has found the Splendid Spur!"

She broke off, and clapp'd her hands together very merrily; and then, as a tear started—

"But thou'lt come for me, ere long, Jack? Else I am sure to blame some other woman. Stay—"

She drew off her ring, and slipp'd it on my little finger.

"There's my token! Now give me one to weep and be glad over."

Having no trinkets, I gave my glove: and she kiss'd it twice, and put it in her bosom.

"I have no need of this ring," said I: "for look!" and I drew forth the lock I had cut from her dear head, that morning among the alders by Kennet side, and worn ever since over my heart.

"Wilt marry no man till I come?"

"Now, that's too hard a promise," said she, laughing, and shaking her curls.

"Too hard!"

"Why, of course. Listen, sweetheart—a true woman will not change her mind: but, oh! she dearly loves to be able to! So, bating this, here's my hand upon it—now, fie, Jack! and before all these mariners!—well, then if thou *must*—"

* * * * *

I watch'd her standing in the stern and waving, till she was under the *Godsend's* side: then turn'd, and mounting Molly, rode inland to the wars.

THE END.

Lightning Source UK Ltd.
Milton Keynes UK
UKOW07f1815050415

249121UK00009B/177/P